What People Are Saying About *The Three Minute Meditator*

"The book *Emotional Intelligence* stated the problem. *The Three Minute Meditator* provides a quick and user-friendly solution."

— John Meharg, M.D.

"This book by the well-known harmonica teacher . . . is filled with deep insight that is made all the more effective because it is presented in an entertaining, lighthearted fashion . . . you'll really be able to 'help your mind help you' after putting these methods into practice . . . it tells you enough that you could use it as a guide to meditating for the rest of your life."

— *Meditation Magazine*

"The book is easy to read, entertaining, and brief. It could serve as a basic introduction to meditation, as a handy reference for veteran meditators, or as a gift that friends will relish . . . Though it may seem odd for a harmonica teacher to write a book on meditation, it would be even stranger to remain unchanged after reading *The Three Minute Meditator*."

— *EastWest Journal*

". . . Your book has been a big hit with my meditation students. Some of them are buying two or three copies to share with their friends . . . the book is very 'user-friendly' to beginning meditators, yet it still contains and is based on the fundamental truths and techniques of all the great classical teachings . . . It is obviously the work of a 'practical transcendentalist' with a sense of humor."

— Lloyd Strom, meditation teacher

"A really well-done book. Best I've seen on the subject. My students love it."

— C. Moore, psychology teacher

"Unlike so many contemporary self-help books, yours is practical and works! Two special features are the attractive format and wry humor which overcome our natural inertia and draw us into the substantive text. We are so entranced that we are ordering copies for each of our three grown children for whom this is also 'their kind of book.'"

— Dr. W. Hassler

"I believe that healing the mind is an important part of healing the body. So I've been recommending *The Three Minute Meditator* to all of my patients. It's a wonderfully simple way for anybody, young or old, healthy or not, to integrate meditation into their daily life."

— Dr. M. Barkette, M.D.

"The Three Minute Meditator really helps people deal with stress and be more effective, at home and in the workplace. I've already given copies to all my friends, and some of my co-workers!"

— M. Bernstein, M.P.H., health educator

"As a drug and alcohol-abuse counselor I need to help my clients replace their negative coping behaviors with new and more positive ones. *The Three Minute Meditator* is perfect. It's easy for my clients to use, and gives immediate results!"

— Dana Snyder, C.S.W.

THE

Three
Minute
MEDITATOR

Third Edition

D A V I D   H A R P

With Nina Feldman, Ph.D.

Foreword by
BEN & JERRY

New Harbinger Publications

Publisher's Note

This publication is designed to provide accurate and authoritative information in regard to the subject matter covered. It is sold with the understanding that the publisher is not engaged in rendering pyschological, financial, legal, or other professional services. If expert assistance or counseling is needed, the services of a competent professional should be sought.

Copyright © 1996 David Harp
New Harbinger Publications, Inc.
5674 Shattuck Avenue
Oakland, CA 94609

Text design by Tracy Marie Powell.

Distributed in U.S.A. by Publishers Group West; in Canada by Raincoast Books; in Great Britain by Airlift Book Company, Ltd.; in South Africa by Real Books, Ltd.; in Australia by Boobook; in New Zealand by Tandem Press.

Library of Congress Catalog Card Number: 96-067942

ISBN 1-57224-054-7 paperback

Printed in the United States of America on recycled paper.

New Harbinger Publications' Web site address: www.newharbinger.com

Second Edition
31,000 copies

99   98

10   9   8   7   6   5   4   3

Contents

Loss and Bereavement   161

*What Is Loss • On Working with Bereavement • The Loss-Labeling Exercise
• The Experiencing Loss Meditation: Practice • The Experiencing Loss
Meditation: In Real Life • Compassion and Bereavement • Bereavement and
Mind Watching • The Waves of Grief • Stages of Grief • Time of Healing,
Healing of Time • Bereavement and the Meditator's Worldview • Loss, Grief,
and The Master Skill*

Loneliness and Emptiness   169

*What Is Loneliness? • The Loneliness-Labeling Exercise • The Experiencing
Loneliness Meditation: Practice • The Experiencing Loneliness Meditation:
In Real Life • Loneliness and Judgment • Working with Loneliness
• Lonlieness: The Compassion Button • What Is Emptiness? • The
Emptiness-Labeling Exercise • The Experiencing Emptiness Meditation:
Practice • The Experiencing Emptiness Meditation:In Real Life • Working
with Emptiness . . . As Lack of Meaning • . . . As Lack of Spiritual
Connectedness . . . As Lack of Inner Self • Loneliness, Emptiness, and
the Master Skill*

Control Issues   175

*"What Is Control"? • Types of Control Issues • Identifying Control-Need
Situations • The Experiencing Control Needs Meditation: Practice • Beliefs
About Control • Is "Control" a Dirty Word? • Two General Control Issues
• Compassion and the Need to Control • Control Needs and the "Don't
Know"• Control and the Master Skill*

Codependency   181

*What Is Codependency? • Codependent Thoughts and Feelings and the
Codependence Phobia • Compassionate Control • Identifying
Codependent-Need Situations • The Experiencing Codependent Thoughts
and Feelings Meditation: Practice • Codependence and Thought Chains
• The Compassionate Codependent Control Button • Dealing with
Codependent Emotions: Real Life • Codependency and the Master Skill*

The Rest Is Up to You   187

Bibliography   189

Other Books by David Harp

Instant Blues Harmonica
Instant Flute
Instant Guitar
Make Me Musical: Harmonica for Kids
Instant Blues and Rock Harmonica Video
Bending the Blues
Harmonica Positions
How to Whistle Like a Pro
Instant Chromatic Harmonica
EarthCards
Instant Rhythm Kit
Music Theory Made Easy
Three Minutes to Blues Harmonica Video
The Pocket Harmonica Songbook
How to Play C&W Harp
Zen and the Art of Blues Harmonica

And with Dr. Nina Feldman

MetaPhysical Fitness
The Three Minute Meditator Audiocassette

Also from David Harp

Instant Blues Harmonica, or *Zen and the Art of Blues Harp Blowing*: book, 96-minute cassette and high-quality harmonica, $16.95

Instant Flute: book and flageolet-style flute, $14.95

Instant Harmonica for Kids: (ages 5-9) entertaining 30-minute video and high-quality harmonica, $14.95 (See David in lots of costumes.)

Instant Guitar: book and 98-minute cassette, $14.95

Three Minutes to Blues Harmonica: 70-minute video and high-quality harmonica, $19.95—results guaranteed within three minutes, really!

Instant Rhythm Kit: book, 60-minute cassette and drumsticks, $9.95

All products guaranteed! Add $4.00 shipping and handling on domestic orders. Foreign orders add $6.00. Check, M.O. or VISA/MC/AmEx accepted. To order, please call either our automated order line (800) 665-6474 or write to us for a brochure at:

Musical I Press
P.O. Box 1561
Montpelier, VT 05602

Ben & Jerry's Foreword

Hi—we're Ben and Jerry. Our pal David asked us to write a fore-word for his newest book, so that's just what we're doing. And if you think it's strange that a couple of guys who make ice cream for a living are writing a foreword for a book like this . . . well, then you probably shouldn't be reading a meditation book written by a harmonica teacher in the first place!

Seriously, though, Harp is probably the best harmonica teacher in the world today, and his strongest talent is teaching other people to do things that he's had to struggle to learn himself. When we were back in high school, he barely knew which end of a kazoo to blow into. Twenty years later, he's taught us (and tons of other unmusical folk) to play harmonica, flute, and guitar. We may never play Carnegie Hall but even playing a little is better than not being able to play at all . . . though Jerry's wife might not agree! We may never get to be full-fledged gurus, either. But learning to use some simple meditation techniques in your daily life sure can't hurt!

So what do you say in a foreword? What's the difference between a foreword, an introduction, and a preface? Does any-body really know? Does it matter? But foreword, backward, or sideways, we're Harpo fanatics. Our only problem is where to begin. Let's see . . . Harp stories, maybe?

Well, we could tell you all about the time Harpo and Jerry spent the night in that haunted house down in Mississippi, but if we did you'd never go to sleep with the light off again. Or the story of how the briny deep claimed Ben's glasses and bar mitzvah ring (Ben's Mom never quite forgave Dave for that one, but hey—she should've just been glad that Ben didn't drown!). Or that amazing seventy-mile-per-hour ice-skid at 4 A.M. outside of Buffalo. Harp claims that he saved our lives then, but if he hadn't been driving we wouldn't have been in danger in the first place.

However, as amusing as these episodes might be, they don't really represent a newer side of our old buddy. The side that does volunteer work with terminally ill children and grieving adults. The side that brought him back to college for his master's degree in psychology. The side that led to the publication of this book . . .

Dave never used to be what you would call a "mellow" type of guy. Smart, definitely. Articulate, without doubt. Mellow, maybe when he was asleep. So we were kind of surprised when he started getting into this meditation stuff for relaxation a couple of years ago. And we were even more surprised when it seemed to be working!

Wine, women, and whatever else he could get away with used to be his main and macho ways of trying to feel good about himself. Plus, he had to be right all the time, even if that meant making you wrong. Going from hyper "up" moods to bummed-out "downs" was just part of a typical Harp day, and he'd sure let his friends know all about how he felt, in detail, like it or not.

But things are a bit different, today. Don't get us wrong—even though he plays a harp, Dave's no angel, not yet anyways. Compared to Mahatma Gandhi or Mother Teresa, the guy still looks pretty funky. Compared to Conan the Barbarian, or Doonesbury's Uncle Duke, he's pretty together. But comparing him to others, whether saints or scoundrels, doesn't mean much. We can only compare him now to the way he was before meditation. And in the words of another old friend, The Durst:

"Hanging out with Dave used to feel like being right smack in the path of a hurricane. Now it's only like walking into a strong wind."

We've got to agree with that. Meditating has been good for the Harp. He likes himself better. He's happier, more secure, and more fun to be with—even when forcing us to try some of the Three Minute Meditations he was writing up for this book.

Actually, the ones we've tried have been fun, and interesting. Jerry did the Breath-Counting Meditation, and got married the next day. Ben did the Flame Concentration with a candle on the table in an Italian restaurant, and had a great dinner within minutes!

So check out *The Three Minute Meditator*. It's cheaper than therapy, easier than living in a cave in the Himalayas—and if it can work for Harp, it can work for you, too!

Ben & Jerry
Vermont
Fall 1987

Acknowledgments

I would like to thank two groups of people for their help and inspiration:

They are, firstly, my teachers and mentors. Some, like Stephen and Ondrea Levine and Jack Kornfield, have gifted me with their spriritual guidance. Others, like Charles Garfield, Matthew McKay, and Stephen Bank, have furnished me with role models and training in my role as a counselor. Others still, such as Karl Scheibe, the late Robert Knapp, Nina Menrath, and Larry Horowitz, have helped to provide me with the academic background necessary to produce even a simple book like this.

They are, secondly, my clients. From the Shanti Project in the late 1970s to the Haight Ashbury Free Clinic in the early 1980s to the Marin County Grief Project and other organizations for whom I now do some volunteer counseling—my clients have taught me the value of opening my heart. From its bottom, I thank them today.

I must also thank my partner, Rita Ricketson, for her indispensable help and support (and for Katie and Lily, too).

Introduction

It's now been eleven years since I participated in the Stephen Levine/Jack Kornfield meditation retreat that so changed every aspect of my life. And I can still say, just as I did in the introduction to the 1990 edition of this book, how consistently beneficial the simple techniques of this book are to me, when I make time to do them diligently. And when I don't, the pain generated by a meditatively impaired life soon reminds me to mend my indolent ways.

Perhaps indolence is the wrong word, since it often seems that I neglect meditating when I'm at my busiest. And with two young children, my harmonica book publishing business, my new instructional video production duties, and my growing "Zen and the Art of Blues Harmonica" speaking career, it's easy to forget to make time, even three minutes' worth, for meditation.

But as I said, pain—the unavoidable pain of seeing my friends, pets, and relatives die, the pain of the business "downs" that follow every "up", or any other variety—eventually reminds me that there is a single cure for all ills. And I know what it is, whether I practice it or not, at any given time. That cure is the ability to see one's own thoughts as objects passing across the screen of the mind, and to deal with them skillfully. The way to gain this ability is through the practice of meditation.

The more I learn about the mind—both from my own experience, and by studying other research, like the research described in Daniel Goleman's fascinating new book, *Emotional Intelligence*, the more I believe in the validity and importance of having an ongoing meditation practice. And I sincerely believe that reading my simple book today can help you learn to make better friends with your own mind, as writing it has helped me to do with mine. Of course, neither reading nor writing is any substitution for doing the work of meditation! Thus, I'll cut this new introduction short, and let you move on to the important stuff! So skim my 1990 introduction, check out Ben & Jerry's foreword, and move on to the Read This First chapter, which will have you up and meditating in no time at all!

David Harp
Montpelier, Vermont
Spring, 1996

The 1990 Introduction

It's been nearly six years since I took the ten day meditation seminar that changed my life so completely, and nearly three since I wrote the first edition of this book. So it's very satisfying to be able to say that everything I've written here about the benefits of meditation seems even truer today (or at least better proven) than ever.

I also believe even more strongly than ever in the concept of "MetaPhysical Fitness"—the idea that meditating is similar to physical fitness in that you have to work at either one of them continuously if you want to stay in good mental or good physical shape. I helped to prove this quite convincingly to myself, in two recent situations, which I'll describe in Part Three.

Many tens of thousands of copies of *The Three Minute Meditator* have been sold to date, and I've received a great deal of feedback on the book. Although most of its fans value it highly, and keep a copy on their bedside table (or, alternately, on top of their toilet tank), quite a number have written to ask exactly how to integrate the meditations into daily life—in other words, how to *use* them.

My twin sister and co-author, Dr. Nina Feldman, and I have addressed these concerns quite explicitly in our new book, *Meta-Physical Fitness: The Complete 30-Day Plan for Your Mental, Emotional, and Spiritual Health* which provides a day-by-day approach to meditation with lots of suggestions for "real-life use." And in this revision of *The Three Minute Meditator,* I have also expanded on ways of integrating the use of meditation into real-life situations.

With this in mind, I've added an all new Part Three to the book, which is composed of sections on using meditation to work with eight specific problem areas. These problem areas (chosen after consultation with my old friends and new publishers at New Harbinger) are: Tension (and Relaxation), Anger, Self-Acceptance (or the lack thereof), Fears and Phobias, Loss and Grief, Feelings of Loneliness and Emptiness.

Other than Part Three, I've resisted the urge to rewrite. I still like *The Three Minute Meditator,* just as it is—because it works. Writing the book has helped me to become a happier and more satisfied person, and I hope that reading it will help you. But neither writing nor reading alone will get either of us very far—*doing* the meditations is what makes all the difference. And that's exactly what I'd like to help you learn to do, right now!

David Harp
San Francisco
Summer 1990

Read This First

I used to be a pretty unhappy guy. I may have looked successful and popular to other people, especially those who didn't know me well. But inside I was vain, insecure, and prone to depression; compulsive about nearly everything, and a hypochondriac to boot. My thoughts and feelings seemed to control me, rather than the other way around . . .

It's no exaggeration to say that learning to meditate has transformed my life. Although my life is still far from perfect, every time I meditate, my ability to handle my old fears and desires grows stronger. My relationships with friends and family become more loving and less critical. I like myself better. And I'm beginning—for the first time in over thirty-five years—to feel some minimal control over that mysterious, mutinous creature called the mind.

I'm No Guru

I'm not a guru. I don't levitate, walk on fire (or water) or materialize Rolls-Royces. I am a highly experienced teacher and writer of instructional books. And whenever I learn to do something, I like to teach it, in the simplest way possible, so as to offer "immediate gratification" to my students.

In the past twelve years I've taught many tens of thousands of people to play the blues harmonica, and have written instructional books about a variety of musical instruments. In the process, I've learned a lot about how people learn. Perhaps my most important finding is that most people would prefer learning to perform some skill "a little bit" right away, rather than taking a long time to learn to do it well. Big surprise!

I realize that there are thousands of psychologists, philosophers, and metaphysicians who have already written books on the subject of meditation. But most of these are not for the beginning, would-be meditator. *After* you've learned to meditate, you'll find many of these books to be fascinating reading. A number of my favorite titles are listed in the bibliography.

Why Many Meditation Books Are Hard to Use

Some meditation books are unbelievably complex—full of long words and torturous, tortuous, concepts. When I began to study meditation, even such useful phrases and concepts like "manifestation of the unpotentiated noumenon" or "nididhyasana sadhana" seemed like a turn-off to me.

But you don't need to know lots of big words to meditate. That's like asking someone to learn Chinese so that they can play Chinese checkers! Once you understand the basic concepts, meditation is a simple thing to do—though not always easy. So there's no need to complicate a beginner's book with strange and esoteric jargon or terminology.

And some meditation books are dogmatic. According to them, there is just one "right" way to meditate. Not surprisingly, the "right" way is usually tied in to a particular religious, social, or business organization, with which the writer is affiliated. Any other method is considered ineffective at best, if not downright sinful.

Over the years, I've read many of these two types of meditation books—the overly complex and the overly orthodox—and learned a great deal from them. But I've especially learned that I prefer my meditation straight: no jargon or cults, and hold the dogma, please!

Not All Meditation Methods Are Alike—but Many Are Similar

While studying many of the available "enlightenment" methods, I found that most share certain characteristics. And I'll try to present these ideas, exercises, and techniques to you as clearly as possible, drawing the concepts together and elaborating on important themes. After all, why should you, as a beginning meditator, have to wade through piles of jargon and dogmatic writings, if I'm willing to act as an interpreter for you? Of course, you can (and should) always go back to the metaphysical literature and explore your areas of special interest, *after* you've learned to meditate. You'll be better prepared to do it then, and my bibliography will help you to do so.

Contrary to popular belief, the study of meditation does not have to be difficult, painful, or other-worldly. You don't have to "pay your dues" by struggling to obtain a meditative consciousness. In fact, struggling is not what this book is about, because I believe that meditation should be an exciting new skill to learn, a skill that has a natural, satisfying, flow of its own!

How This Book Is Arranged

Although this book is action-oriented, I plan to include a certain amount of the theory and philosophy of meditation. I've arranged the book so that much of the basic theory appears in Part One. The most important paragraphs of this theoretical information are boxed, like the one on the next page. Thus people who want to go right to the Three Minute Meditation Exercises can still get the gist of the theory sections by reading just the boxed chunks.

Part Two is pretty much self-explanatory. The opening chapters discuss the ins and outs of guruhood, my concept of "Meta-Physical Fitness," and how to use the actual exercises. Various theoretical and historical explanations also precede each of the exercise groups.

Part Three explains how to apply the theoretical information of Part One and the exercises of Part Two to some specific problem areas that we all face.

That's all there is to it, friends. I believe that if you give meditation a sincere try, you'll find it as helpful and satisfying as I do, and it will become a lifelong practice.

The Box Method

If you're in a big rush to begin meditating, you can read only the boxed sections. As you skim through the pages, going from one box to the next, look at each boldface section title as well, and read any section that particularly appeals to you. This will get you to the first meditation exercise, and then through Part One, in no time at all! Then, after you've gotten a few more of the Three Minute Meditations from Part Two under your mental belt, you can go back and read the rest of Part One at your leisure, or go on to Part Three for specific ways to apply the meditations.

What Is Meditation?

Meditation is the art of mental self-control. Each of the Three Minute Meditations in this book is an *exercise* that will help you understand and gain control over your mind and your thoughts.

Why You Probably Need to Meditate

Are you ever bothered by anger or fear? Distracted by desires? Depressed, bored, or restless? Does life sometimes seem meaningless? Are you only able to feel happy when everything is going right?

If you never have problems with feelings like these, then you probably don't need this book. You're probably not human, either, since just about everybody manages to make themselves unhappy at least once in a while.

"Make themselves unhappy?" What a strange notion! Why would anybody want to make themselves unhappy?

Of course, it's much easier to believe that circumstances, or other people, make us unhappy. But that's a load of baloney! Because we've all met, or at least read and heard about, those few rare people who are able to be happy no matter what adversity shows up in their life. And we can all name a dozen rich, famous, healthy people whose lives were made miserable by themselves, from John Belushi to Howard Hughes. Make ourselves unhappy? You bet we do!

It's not really what happens in the outside world that makes a person happy or unhappy, satisfied or unsatisfied. What matters is how you feel inside your own mind. During the 1929 Stock Market Crash, many of the brokers who dove to their deaths from Wall Street windows had more than enough money left to maintain a modest lifestyle. The stock market didn't kill them, and the window didn't kill them. Their own minds did.

You see, for most of us, the mind can often be a cruel and demanding master, constantly criticizing and making judgments. It churns out a storm of contradictory, confusing thoughts. Makes you buy that 1997 GarbonzoMobile on credit, and then worry about the monthly payments. Makes you eat that extra helping, and then obsess about being overweight. Lets you forget about an anniversary date, but reminds you of the time you accidentally wore a pajama top to class in second grade. Makes you feel angry about demands from your child or parent, and then feel guilty for not being the "perfectly giving" father or mother, daughter or son. Jobs, sex, money, health—the list of potentially disturbing thoughts that your mind is just aching to throw at you goes on and on. But it doesn't need to be that way.

Your mind doesn't have to be a weight around (or, rather, on top of) your neck. Meditation, the art of mental self-control, can quite literally "change your mind"—from a pain-in-the-butt boss to a useful and lively companion! Why let your own mind continue to work against you, when you can train it to work *for* you?

Why I Needed to Meditate

My own transformation into a Three Minute Meditator illustrates the way in which you can use meditation to shift from an "armed camp" relationship with your own mind to a peaceful and interesting coexistence.

My mind used to be a judgmental, nit-picking boss, and my life generally felt great when absolutely every little thing was going my way, or when something especially satisfying had just happened, and awful the rest of the time. I spent a lot of time feeling depressed, for no obvious reasons. But that was how it had always been for me, and I had no reason to think that things should, or even could, be different.

In 1984, things changed. I was about to publish the first nationally marketable edition of my *Instant Blues Harmonica for the 'Musical Idiot'!* package, of which I was enormously proud. But while my book was at the printers, a larger publisher (whom I had trusted, and taught to play harmonica) came out with his own version, with a distressingly similar title! My own brainchild, I felt, had been kidnapped, and I was terribly angry, hurt, scared, and depressed.

But, in my acute misery, a single healthy thought kept recurring: the idea that if I could somehow learn the "master skill" of *coping* with a situation like this, that skill would ultimately be worth more to me than a dozen successfully published harmonica books.

That thought persevered. I bought psychology, philosophy, and metaphysical books, and read and reread them slowly and carefully. Previously, I had read these books for entertainment, or to learn the newest (and hippest) theories. Now, it felt like I was reading for my very life.

Virtually all of my favorite books strongly recommended some sort of daily meditation practice, so I began, after a twelve-year hiatus, to experiment again with the Transcendental Meditation™ technique that I'd learned but never really practiced in college. I also signed up for a ten-day meditation retreat with psychologist/poet Stephen Levine and Buddhist teacher Jack Kornfield, where I learned that a tremendous diversity of meditation techniques exist.

I began to study meditation, and to make it a part of my daily life. As I learned some "mental self-control," my own thought processes became clearer to me. I found myself slightly less dominated by the usual old feelings of fear and desire. Hypochondria, my favorite bugaboo, would still surface occasionally, but I would generally recognize it quickly and let go of it. My previous day-long or week-long depressions began to disappear in seconds or minutes, hours at most. And even the insecurities that had obsessed me since grammar school started to fade quietly into the background noise of my mind.

I surely don't mean to imply that I'm really together now. I'd better not! Firstly, because it's not true, and secondly, because if I did, and my friends ever read this, I'd face a barrage of well-deserved ridicule, just as I did when *PM Magazine* did a TV segment on me and called it (their idea, *not* mine) "The Harmonica Guru"!

But I am more together than before I began meditating. Today, outside events affect me less, and I can understand and deal with my thoughts and feelings much more easily.

I believe in meditation. I believe that it's been good for me, and I believe that it will help you, too. And that's why I wrote this book.

Emotional Intelligence and Meditation

As I said in the introduction, Daniel Goleman's popular book, *Emotional Intelligence* (1995), has given me new and improved scientific reasons for my belief in the importance of meditation. The book never mentions meditation (there isn't even an entry under that word in the index). But it provides a comprehensive, scientific, and entertaining look at why our thoughts, feelings, and even actions so often seem outside of our conscious control—as well as why learning to control them is so critically important.

Goleman's book states that: "Self-awareness—recognizing a feeling as it happens—is the keystone of emotional intelligence. . . . Handling feelings so they are appropriate is an ability that builds on self-awareness." As you will soon see, this concept of "recognizing and handling feelings" fits in perfectly with my definition of meditation as "the art of mental self-control," in which we respectively learn to "clear" the mind, watch our thoughts and feelings, and, ultimately, bring them more under our conscious control.

So in this new edition of *The Three Minute Meditator*, I decided to include the metaphor of emotional intelligence for a number of reasons. One reason, I admit, is that *Emotional Intelligence* has proven to be a very popular book. Another is that the concept of emotional intelligence (developed by psychologists Peter Salovey and John Mayer about five years ago) is very "nuts and bolts" oriented: that is, it refers to the immediately observable mental skills that make some of us so much happier and more successful than others in every realm of human endeavor.

It's not that I don't like high-flying metaphysical systems, angels, gurus, and celestial prophecies as much as the next guy (if the next guy is Sri Nisargaddata). But reading about such satisfying but unsubstantial entities usually doesn't change the way you think—or the way you relate to the world and its inhabitants—nearly as effectively as even a minimal meditation practice does. Although this edition of *The Three Minute Meditator* still includes a number of sections that might be called spiritual or metaphysical (and I think that they are useful to read, for inspiration, at the least), my own emphasis these days, in my personal life and my counseling practice, is on working more skillfully with thoughts, feelings, and the actions that they precede—via the art of meditation, naturally. Besides, just as a serious golfing habit will increase your general fitness, whether you are doing it for that purpose or not, I believe that a good meditation habit will increase your metaphysical fitness, like it or not!

Perhaps you are wondering: If I like the book *Emotional Intelligence* so much, how come I don't just recommend that you read it, and save a bunch of trees by ending *this* book right here? Why not? Because *Emotional Intelligence*, in my opinion, is a book with a fatal flaw. It admirably describes an important problem—the all-too-human lack of control over the mind—but it does not provide much of an answer. And for me, of course, meditation is the answer to the problem of emotional intelligence (or, rather, its lack). So let's learn how to do it!

But for those of us who like to know *why* things work as they do, here's some historical and physiological information about the underpinnings of meditation. For those of you who are more experientially oriented, please skim your way on to the next box.

Dinosaur Brain, Modern Mind

For me, the first part of *Emotional Intelligence* was the most exciting. Goleman begins by describing how our modern human brain has developed, since dinosaur days, into the powerful, complex, contradictory tool that it now is (as have many others, like Paul McLean and Willis Harmon). He then discusses (and here's the exciting part) how the use of advanced computer "scanning" equipment allows neurologists to identify how the various parts of the brain, old and new, are involved in different mental processes, and how nerve "circuits" and "hormone-based" circuits connect these parts.

A Vast Oversimplification

The following is a brief and vastly oversimplified explanation of how the human brain and mind came to be as they are. You don't need this information in order to meditate, but understanding some of the background of the brain may help you appreciate the process of meditation more fully.

Hundreds of millions of years ago, the ancestors of our ancestors were small, land-dwelling reptiles, not far removed from those adventurous fish who left the water to crawl with their fins along the beach. What passed for brains in their pointy little heads ran mostly on instincts—smell-based instincts—which told them whom to eat, run from, or mate with. This "nose-brain" (more politely called, in Latin, the *rhinencephalon*) was the forerunner of our own three pounds of gray matter.

Tree Swingers and the Developing Brain

By the time, many tens of millions of years ago, our indirect ancestors left the ground to swing amongst the treetops, their brains had already begun to develop in a way that affects us to this day. Layers of cells (now called the "limbic system") surrounded the nose-brain, and gave the tree swingers rudimentary capabilities of memory and even learning. If playing with those seemingly innocent little black-and-white striped creatures resulted in a nose-burning stench, then those creatures could be remembered, and avoided, in the future.

The next step in brain power involved seeing rather than smelling. Basically, the tree swingers needed to be able to make instantaneous decisions about what to grab next. After all, mistaking a tree trunk or a large leaf for the limb of a tree would be a serious mistake when attempting to travel from branch to branch.

So their brains began to evolve the ability to recognize important objects instantly. Their eyes would scan an object, and if it generally looked more like a branch than a leaf or a tree trunk, their brain would give them an instantaneous go-ahead to grab it, without taking time for even the marginal amount of thinking that they were capable of. More layers of brain cells were added to surround the nose-brain, eventually developing into the modern "neocortex": the thinking brain. And, perhaps, the first manifestation of what might be called thoughts came about, in what someday would be called "The Mind"!

As the mammalian brain continued to enlarge, and our predecessors evolved towards humanhood, the brain maintained and expanded upon this habit of making quick decisions based on comparing outside realities with pictures produced instantaneously within the mind. We now know, from CAT scans and the like, that a primitive, "limbic," part of the brain called the "amygdala" appears to be in charge of this function.

Primitive humans, like other animals, also had to make decisions—most importantly, whether to fight or flee when another creature suddenly appeared. Deciding to flee from a flamingo would result in the loss of a meal, while deciding to fight a bear would result in death. Instead of making an exhaustive analysis in cases like these, the brain learned to leap to conclusions. These conclusions were based on mental images implanted in the brain, which would be triggered by the general size and shape of certain visible objects. *After* reacting instantly, the object, or approacher, could then be examined in more careful detail, and from a safer distance.

In effect, then, our prehistoric forebears were learning to *react physically to mental images*. Many a caveman, unexpectedly perceiving a tree stump at dusk, doubtless jumped for cover as his mind flashed him a mental image of a stalking tiger. Shortly afterwards, comparing tiger image to stump reality, he perhaps felt embarrassed, but if he hadn't jumped, and it *had* been a tiger . . .

Fight or Flight . . . in Fantasy

Recent neurological discoveries lend great weight to the theory that the way our brain developed now causes us to react to a thought, a mental image, as though it were an actual, visual image. Thus, as we walk down a dark city street, the *thought* of a mugger lurking in the next doorway (and the instantaneous accompanying mental image) causes us to react physiologically in much the same way as the sighting of an *actual* mugger.

The entire nervous system mobilizes its resources, adrenaline and other hormones rush through our body, blood pressure increases, and we feel anxious, as the "fight-or-flight" response is triggered.

Reacting Without Thinking

All this happens almost instinctively—processed, at least initially, by the ancient nose-brained amygdala that continues to reside in each of our skulls. It even appears that our brains are still "wired" so that our muscles and hormonal systems can react without actually thinking: that is, our physical reaction takes place based on input solely from the amygdala long before our more rational neocortex is even aware of a real or imagined threat.

Fight or Flight . . . in Memory

Neurological research also indicates that, perhaps as a remnant of the ancient "limbic system" style of memory and learning, *memories* of important events ("Uh oh, black-and-white striped guy made me stink for weeks.") can produce the same physical reactions the actual incident did. So the thought of a skunk—if you've had an emotionally charged experience with one—will instantly and unconsciously cause your muscles to tense and your adrenaline to flow, just as seeing the real thing would. In fact, seeing a black and white cat may even bring the same reaction, as your limbic brain jumps to a conclusion based on just a partial match of information, and you react to "skunk" long before your conscious mind, with its rational neocortex, points out the longer legs and thinner tail. Or, for a more up-to-date example: The sight of someone with the same prehistoric build and swaggering walk as your much-feared high school bully—though only a partial match, since it's not really him—may trigger a fight-or-flight reaction. And worst of all, as adrenaline and other stress hormones surge through your body, you may not even realize that the glance at an unknown oaf was what caused you to feel anxious all afternoon.

A Life of Constant Stress

Thus the thought of a nuclear war, memory of an auto accident or abusive ex-spouse, the image of the boss approaching with a pink slip in hand—or any other emotionally negative thought or memory (even a close match to one)—can cause our body to react with the classic fight-or-flight response. No wonder many of us therefore spend a large part of each day in a state of chronic readiness for escape or battle. Perhaps a useful state in the predator-ridden prehistoric world, it is an unnecessary burden in our current society's (mostly) less threatening environment.

Neural Hijacking and Neural Static

These habitual fight-or-flight reactions, implemented by ancient and often unconscious parts of our brain, cause two problems in addition to excess stress: Goleman calls these "neural hijacking" and "neural static."

Neural hijackings are situations in which limbic-system reactions cause us to fly into the rage or fear reactions, which, upon later and more rational reflection, seem so inappropriate and sudden—and the most extreme of which could easily land us in trouble, jail, or even the hospital or the morgue.

Less drastic, but still highly inconvenient, is neural static. Neural static refers to the unpleasant state in which you are trying to concentrate on something—whether a career decision or a math test—and emotional thoughts prevent you from doing so.

Dinosaurs, Meditators, and Emotional Intelligence: Briefly

Our current model brain developed over hundreds of millions of years, and still contains some pretty old components. Some of these old parts, dating back to dinosaur times, cause us to have intense muscular and hormonal reactions (known as the fight-or-flight response) to thoughts and memories as well as actual events. Many folds thus spend a large part of each day in an inappropriate state of readiness for escape or battle. And this takes an unnecessary toll in many different ways. Want more detail? Read the entire section above, or the book *Emotional Intelligence*, when you get a chance.

Why Meditate?

In addition to the problems of neural hijacking and neural static, even more unhealthy effects of excess stress—often caused by that chronic fight-or-flight state—have been chronicled over the last fifty years. Goleman cites dozens of studies that prove the negative results of not being able to control anger, anxiety, or depression in the workplace, in school, in marriage, and in the parent-child bond. He cites many more studies that show the relationship between the inability to control your thoughts and feelings and health, both mental and physical.

Fortunately, an equal but opposite reaction to the fight-or-flight response also exists, known as the "relaxation response"; it balances the anxiety of the fight-or-flight response by calming and relaxing the nervous system. It has been scientifically proven that a particular type of meditation, which I call Clearing the Mind, is the most effective method of producing the relaxation response. For more clinical evidence on this subject, read Dr. Herbert Benson's book, *The Relaxation Response* (see bibliography).

The relaxation response is only one of the benefits of meditation. As I've just described, although our thoughts can have a tremendous effect on us, this effect does not have to be a negative one. And if we learn to observe, understand, and control the thoughts that unceasingly flow through our minds, we can turn this potentially negative effect into a positive one. We can reduce the likelihood of neural hijacking and catch ourselves sooner if it does begin to arise. We can notice and then turn down the volume of neural static, and learn to focus our mental attention when, where, and for how long we choose. We can become more aware, effective, relaxed, and loving human beings. This is the purpose of meditation.

Meditation: The Benefits

If you know enough about meditation to even pick up a book with a title like this one, chances are that you already know that meditation is full of benefits. It will calm you down and help you deal with the stresses of daily life by teaching you to observe and then control your thoughts and feelings. It will probably allow you to sleep less, while increasing your available energy. It can be used to lower your blood pressure and heart rate. Meditation will help you appreciate life more, and face change or loss with greater acceptance and compassion.

Knowing about all these benefits, how could anybody not meditate? There are three simple answers: excuses, excuses, excuses!

Excuses, Excuses, Excuses!

Yes, there are reasons not to meditate. But they are not good reasons. If you think you have reasons for not meditating, please read the following section and take the "Why I Don't Meditate" test. I believe that it will help you see how erroneous beliefs about meditation are preventing you from enjoying one of the world's oldest and most useful forms of self-help!

The "Why I Don't Meditate" Test

The late sixties through the late seventies saw a tremendous upsurge of interest in the quest for "inner peace." If you were in college during those times, or if you even opened a newspaper during that decade, you were no doubt exposed to many highly visible quests for enlightenment. The Beatles went to India, Shirley MacLaine went to Peru, and whole planeloads of disciples followed Maharaj Ji, the fifteen-year-old "Perfect Master," around the United States on tour (until his mother called him home, for exhibiting conduct unbecoming to a guru).

However, many members of this generation of enlightenment-seekers have since dropped their search. Others of us may never have had the motivation—or the time or the money—to indulge in such a venture of the spiritual sort. Although we may have thought longingly in private that there "just might be something to that," it probably seemed easier to view it all as a fad or affectation and laugh it off with, "What will those people do next?" And certainly the well-publicized incidents of guru misconduct made it easier to discount the entire subject of spiritual searching.

Unfortunately, many who have developed a "not me" orientation towards meditation are those who could benefit from it the most. But feelings of resistance may prevent them from doing so.

Other people who could benefit from a daily meditation practice just can't quite find the energy or motivation to begin. The hardest part of beginning your meditation practice is just that—beginning! But the following test should help . . .

As I mentioned earlier, there are books out there to get you started—perhaps not all are as useful as they could be, but they do exist—and various methods for training meditators have been available for centuries. Perhaps you've even started and stopped meditating once already, as so many did with Transcendental Meditation™. But regardless of whether you've never tried to meditate, or whether you've tried before without continued success, the next section will help you to get started—today!

Dr. N. S. Feldman and the "Would-Be Meditator" Syndrome

Dr. Nina Feldman is a Princeton-trained psychologist, Transcendental Meditation™ dropout, and college graduate of the early seventies whose self-professed goal at one time was to "wear flowing white robes and float about two inches off the ground." Of course, that was *before* she went to Princeton.

Nina and I have known each other for a long time and have worked together previously on a number of projects. Our earliest collaboration involved the decision as to whether myself or twin sister Nina would be the eldest child in our family of four. I won out by ten minutes. In spite of that incontrovertible fact, Nina has ever since insisted on referring to me as her baby brother, her rationale being that, "in previous lives, I bet that I must have been the firstborn!"

All joking aside, ten years ago Nina's expertise in psychology and experimental testing combined with my interest in teaching music to people who considered themselves unmusical or even tone-deaf. We developed a test to help people discover the roots of their musical blockage.

The insights offered by this test were so useful that we decided to use this same approach to help would-be meditators explore their own "meditational blockage." In doing so, Nina conducted many interviews with would-be meditators around the country and found a remarkable consistency in their reasons for an "approach/avoidance" (I want to meditate/I'm not making any attempt to do so) conflict.

The following quiz is designed to help you explore your own meditational blockage. This test is not intended to predict how motivated a meditator you will become or how useful the effects will be for you. The answers to those questions will only come over time. It can, however, help you understand and overcome the excuses which may have prevented you from exploring your own meditation potential.

As you take this quiz, recognize that there are no right or wrong answers. Please be as honest as possible. Simply write whether you agree or disagree with each of the following statements. Those of you who do *not* feel blocked in your investigation of meditation may wish to skip this test.

The "Why I Don't Meditate" Test

1. Meditation is not worth doing unless you can devote a lot of time to it.   Agree/Disagree

2. I'm the kind of person who will tense up and not be able to get into meditation.   Agree/Disagree

3. Meditation pulls a lot of people in at first, but most of them seem to drop out. If it *really* worked, people would stick with it.   Agree/ Disagree

4. Meditation takes years of work and practice. A book this simple can't possibly teach me anything.   Agree/Disagree

5. Meditation might work for some people, but it probably won't work for me.   Agree/Disagree

6. I won't have the willpower to stick to a meditation program.   Agree/Disagree

7. People are fooling themselves if they think meditation really makes a difference.   Agree/Disagree

8. My life is too busy to fit meditation into it.

    Agree/Disagree

9. This book looks like the Mickey Mouse version of meditation. I'm better off waiting until I have the time to do the real thing.   Agree/Disagree

The value of this test lies in the four separate themes that your answers will now help you investigate. Please refer back to your answers for the designated questions as you read the following paragraphs. Most people who are would-be meditators will find that at least a few of these erroneous beliefs about meditation are blocking their progress.

The Myth of Innate Ability: Refer to Questions 2, 5, and 6

Many people who foreclose on their own meditative potential share a belief in a widespread and damaging myth. Do *you* believe that "All successful meditators are born with an innate ability to clear their minds, to focus their thoughts, and to concentrate on their inner lives"? If your answer is "yes," you are wrong!

The truth is that *meditators are made, not born.* The ability to meditate is a characteristic that every human being has—an ability that must be nurtured and encouraged in order for it to bear fruit. No matter how tense or unspiritual you now think yourself to be, rewards await you, but only if you try.

Once you begin to believe this, you can turn your wistful *would-be* meditator self-image into a *beginning* meditator self-image, and thus start to enhance your own life with these tremendously useful techniques. Vividly visualizing yourself meditating will help you begin taking the steps to unblock your meditative potential.

Not all of us will have the time or the inclination to spend hours a day meditating. But *anyone* with a sincere desire to meditate can begin to learn and use these techniques *immediately.*

Big Is Beautiful: Refer to Questions 4 and 9

If you think that this book is too simple to teach you anything, then you may be suffering from the "Big Is Beautiful," or rather "Complicated Is Better," syndrome. Why is it that we often need to make things appear complicated, difficult or expensive before we value them?

Much of the beauty of meditation lies in its exquisite simplicity. And simple as they may seem, these Three Minute Meditations are *the* basic tools which anyone who wants to meditate will eventually have to master. If this book makes these tools appear obvious, so much the better!

The fact is that as much or as little as you do, simply *getting started* is what counts. And that's what this book is designed to help you do. Once you've begun, you can then expand your practice of meditation in any direction you choose.

Lack of Time: Refer to Questions 1 and 8

When you view meditation as an exercise which requires clearing a large time slot each day before you can begin, chances are that you will never get started. Today will not seem right and tomorrow will seem even worse. Life is so hectic for many of us that clearing half an hour or so daily may seem like an impossible task. And to think of doing so repeatedly, perhaps even twice a day, may be enough to leave most of us thinking, "Maybe *next* year, when things ease up!"

For those of us who feel pressured by lack of time, meditation is likely always to remain in our vague and distant future. Ironically, the time spent meditating, even three minutes' worth, is often enough to clear the mind so that the rest of the day seems to flow more smoothly, as if time has somehow expanded to meet the needs that arise. This erroneous belief in the time demands of meditation has blocked many a would-be meditator (including, for many years, both myself and Nina!)

Meditation Doesn't Work Anyway: Refer to Questions 3 and 7

Some people believe in the aggressive tenet that "the best defense is a good offense." Attacking the usefulness of meditation is a means through which many who have considered meditating are able to assure themselves that they are not really missing anything by their meditational blockage.

Much of this attack may be based on a pre-programmed sense of failure. Would-be meditators who suffer from this blockage often are asking themselves, "Why even try meditating, since it obviously doesn't work?" Another element of this attack consists of denigrating meditation because everyone who tries it does not continue. Yet this fact may be more of a reflection on ineffective teaching techniques and the unrealistic demands that many disciplines try to impose on busy Westerners than a reflection on the value of meditation itself.

Meditation techniques have been used by members of every major religion since the beginning of recorded history. Meditation has clearly stood the test of time, so if you are using *this* excuse, it's long out of date! Time to give up your excessive skepticism, and become a Three Minute Meditator.

Bringing Meditation into Our Lives

Once you understand the four most common barriers that would-be meditators face, we hope you'll agree with our final analysis, which is: The only thing that now stands between you and meditation is the willingness to begin *right now!*

So let's briefly reconsider the four obstacles. The idea of innate ability is just a myth, because everybody has the God-given ability to meditate. The "Big Is Beautiful" concept is mostly a form of spiritual snobbery, counterproductive although understandable in our highly status-conscious culture. The "Meditation Doesn't Work" justification is strictly sour grapes. Meditation doesn't work only if you don't do it. Finally, "Lack of Time" is no longer an excuse—because the Three Minute Meditator Method demonstrates how meditation can be effectively done in small chunks of time. And, even in small doses, meditation is effective in improving the quality of one's life.

If your goal is realistic ("I will begin learning to clear my mind") rather than perfectionistic ("I must achieve enlightenment right away"), then your progress towards this goal is virtually guaranteed from the outset. All that is necessary is to take a few deep breaths, relax—and continue reading! And breathing, and meditating, as well.

Reading About Swimming

There's an old joke about an intellectual fellow who loved to read. He read all that there was to read about philosophy, and became a philosopher. He read all that there was to read about mathematics, and became a mathematician. Then he read all that there was to read about swimming, and he drowned.

Again, that's the main problem I have with the book *Emotional Intelligence*. It tells you why meditation works on the human brain (with a bit of extrapolating on your part) and why everyone needs to do it, but it doesn't tell you how, and I fear that some people will read that book and think, erroneously, that they've done something to help control their minds. They probably haven't . . . yet.

There are some subjects that you just have to *do* more than *read* about. Meditating is one of them. So even though you may feel that you're not yet very well informed about the subject, right now may be a good time to take three minutes, or even one, and do the meditation on the next page. The instructions are simple and clear, so don't think about it much, just give it a try.

The Breath-Counting Meditation

Begin by practicing this meditation while sitting comfortably in a quiet place, with your back straight, feet flat on floor, hands in lap.

Simply count the exhale of each breath, mentally: "Inhale . . . one, Inhale . . . two, Inhale . . . three, Inhale . . . four" then begin again with "Inhale . . . one." Do it once *now, before* reading any further.

Now continue reading these instructions and try this simple meditation some more. Strive not to lose the count, and also try not to alter or regularize your breathing in any way. See if you can feel the physical sensation of each breath, both the inhale and exhale, as it passes through your nose or mouth. Does this breath feel warm, or cool? Is it a quick breath, or a slow one?

If you find yourself thinking about anything except the feel of your breath and the number of that breath, return to focus on the sensation of breathing, and on the number of the breath. If you are not absolutely sure what number breath you're on, immediately begin again with "Inhale . . . one." No judging, no "I blew the count" thoughts, just back to "Inhale . . . one."

When enjoying a favorite hobby, like making model ships or sewing, your thoughts generally focus directly on just what you're doing. Gluing wood, or stitching, become your "preferred" thoughts. Right now, consider the counting of each breath and how each breath feels to be your "preferred" thoughts. So other thoughts such as memories, plans, fears, desires, lunch, or whatever else will just be gently replaced by your "Inhale . . . one, Inhale . . . two" and so on, as soon as you notice them creeping in. And they will! Of course it's difficult to stay focused, but strangely satisfying, as it becomes more natural.

The beauty of this meditation is that, once learned, you can do it *anywhere!* Try it on the bus, or during a long, boring meeting. Like all "mind-clearing" exercises, with a bit of practice the breathing meditation gives rise to a delightfully peaceful and calm feeling (the relaxation response, if you recall, from page 13). Now do it again, or read on, as you like.

PART I

The Journey Towards Enlightenment

In Part One of this book, I'm going to present some concepts that will help you to understand meditation more clearly and completely. I'll begin by describing a particular way of thinking about the world that almost all long-term meditators eventually seem to adopt. Initially, you may find it difficult to believe in this alternative worldview. But, as you meditate, you will find that it somehow begins to make intuitive sense.

I'll also talk about what is commonly called the "state of enlightenment." Often, people who don't know much about meditation focus exclusively upon this elusive state as the sole "goal" of the beginning meditator. Actually, this mistaken focus upon enlightenment may impede or discourage would-be meditators rather than inspire or assist them. Understanding that enlightenment is more like a journey than a destination is far more useful than grasping greedily at some supposed spiritual goalpost! On this road, each single step is what counts.

I'll end Part One by discussing the three most important "steps on the road" that meditation will help us to discover.

For some of us (myself included), the idea of attaining enlightenment may seem a bit much—just another slice of metaphysical pie-in-the-sky. And it's fine to feel that way, because the main use of meditation is as a practical daily tool with almost instantaneous beneficial results.

A Meditator's Guide
to the Universe

"I Stand Alone": The Western Worldview

Most of us in this workaday Western world tend to hold on to one rather limited but overwhelmingly popular way of relating to ourselves and the world. I'll call this the "Western worldview," and begin by describing the "Western self-image."

When subscribing to the Western worldview, we see ourselves primarily as a body, a few cubic feet of flesh, with a specialized chunk at the top end called a brain. Complex chemical interactions in this brain chunk somehow give rise to instincts, emotions, thoughts, and self-awareness.

We believe that anything inside the skin is "me," anything outside is "not me." This not-me part includes everybody else and everything else, from rocks to raccoons to real estate agents.

"We Are All One": The Meditator's Worldview

But there's more than one way to think of ourselves in relation to the rest of the universe. For thousands of years, mystics and meditators (the two often go together, though they don't have to) of all persuasions have maintained an alternate opinion, which I call the "Meditator's worldview."

In the Meditator's worldview, the universe is, to paraphrase theoretical physicist Sir James Jeans, more like an "enormous mind" than an "enormous machine." And each one of us is more like an integrated thought in a great big mind than like an isolated little cog functioning almost independently in a great big machine (as in the Western view). Some people like to refer to this "big mind" as the universal consciousness. Others prefer to think of it as "God," the "higher power," or the "all-that-is."

Some analogies may help to clarify this concept. If you'd like to explore these worldviews further, please read the Watts and LeShan books listed in the bibliography.

The Dream Analogy

Row, row, row, your boat gently down the stream.
Merrily, merrily, merrily, merrily, life is but a dream.

I'd sung that song, like everybody else, since childhood, without ever really stopping to look for any particular meaning in it. Yet for thousands of years, philosophers of every culture have compared the unenlightened person to a character in a dream, whose understanding of reality is limited to the "reality" of the dream world that he inhabits.

Think about dreaming. In any dream, there are a variety of dream characters. But you'll probably believe yourself to be one particular character—that is, you'll know which character you are in the dream, even though that character might be somewhat different from who you are when awake. I've dreamed of being older, and younger, of being a Russian, and even a Martian. But whoever I am in the dream, I know that it's me, in spite of the fact that my dream character may change from one part of the dream to another.

Yet although I almost never realize it during the dream, my "waking-life-mind" is creating both the "Dave-character-within-the-dream," and the rest of the characters in that dream.

Seen from the Meditator's worldview, we could say that each one of us is now like a dream character in a scenario dreamed by the "big mind." The big mind (or God, or universal consciousness) is dreaming both me, and everyone and everything else in this real-seeming dream that I live in. Since I see this universal dream from my own limited point of view (the Western view), the other people and things in it seem separate from me, although they're not. We are all characters in the same universal dream, dreamed by the mind of God. And it's "just" a dream, no matter how real it feels.

The important element of the Meditator's worldview is that we are each much more than a tiny, isolated mind/body. We are instead a tiny but important part of a collective consciousness which includes all that has ever existed. We've just momentarily lost sight of this fact, when we were born into this culture, with its prevailing Western view.

Invisible Connections

A mushroom growing on the ground appears to be an individual plant. Yet the thumb-sized piece we call the mushroom is actually only a tiny, temporary part of a fungal network (known as a mycelium) that exists underground, year-round, and which may be as large as a football field. Those thousands of mushrooms spread around a meadow, seemingly separate, are all organs or parts of a single organism.

In the Western worldview, a person is like our erroneous concept of the mushroom: tiny, temporary, and isolated. When we switch to the Meditator's worldview, we see the mushroom as an integral part of a mycelium field, and the individual person as an inseparable part of the universal consciousness.

The Cosmic Ocean

A wave in an ocean seems to have an individual identity of its own. It appears, and exists for a while. You can watch it, and listen to it, and surf on it. Then it disappears back into the ocean, of which it was composed. Try thinking of yourself as a wave in the ocean of consciousness.

Please take a moment now to return to page 21 and do the Breath-Counting Meditation.

Your Own Worldview: A Pervasive Perspective

Taking either the Western or the Meditator's approach to life shapes our perceptions of some very basic issues. Attitudes towards birth, death, and everything in-between are affected by our choice of worldview.

Birth

In the Western worldview, birth is seen as a rather mechanical event, combining egg and sperm like two chemicals that mix to form a compound substance with its own particular properties. Consciousness then results from a biochemical reaction in the newly formed brain.

In the Meditator's worldview, some impulse or desire in the big consciousness to express itself in physical reality causes the interactions necessary to bring man and woman together, then sperm and egg. Thus each individual is a "recycled piece" of the universal consciousness.

God

In the Western worldview, God tends to be seen as above and separate from the world. God is the creator of the universe, almost as a person might create and then run a business.

In the Meditator's worldview, God isn't separate from the world, but is the consciousness out of which everything is formed. So God is the entire universe, which includes me, you, Mother Teresa, and Al Capone.

From the Western point of view, when someone says "I am God," it probably means that they are crazy, and they expect everybody else to bow down to them. From the Meditator's point of view, when someone says "I am God," it may mean that they understand that everybody, and everything, is God also, because God is the "stuff" out of which everything, and everybody, is made.

Cause and Effect

In the Western world, each individual performs specific actions that have particular effects on the world. In the Meditator's worldview, everything you do is connected to and dependent on everything else.

Think about your neighbor's cat. Its movements in the neighborhood, in the Western view, seem random, and completely independent of anything else.

Yet, in the Meditator's view, the cat is drawn to one yard because of a honeysuckle bush that attracts hummingbirds, and avoids another yard due to the presence of a large dog. The honeysuckle bush was planted by a family who left the Old Country after an earthquake in the 1880s. The other family bought a watchdog after a neighbor's house was broken into by thieves. In a very real way, the cat's movements today are connected to an earthquake in the past and the fear of potential crime in the future. This same "interconnected" viewpoint applies to any event: political, social, economic, or interpersonal.

Good and Evil

In the Western worldview, events and people that you like are called "good," those you dislike are called "evil." Good and evil are considered absolute terms. It is always possible to tell them apart, and to tell which is which.

In the Meditator's worldview, it's understood that good and evil are relative terms. Each is valid only when considered from a particular point of view. During the Civil War, a Northerner would consider General Grant good, and General Lee evil. A Southerner would think exactly the reverse.

Death

In the Western worldview, death of the body necessarily means death of consciousness, since consciousness is merely a byproduct of the brain's biochemical activities. Even those Western viewers with traditional Judeo-Christian or other religious upbringings may find it difficult to reconcile their religious beliefs about life after death with their beliefs about physiological reality.

In the Meditator's worldview, death means some kind of re-absorption or recycling of us into the universal consciousness. Thus, it is easy and natural to believe in any form of life after physical death, even though the specifics may be presently unknowable. Virtually all of our spiritual leaders, from Moses to Martin Buber and from Jesus to Thomas Merton, have deeply believed in the Meditator's outlook on life after death.

Living in the "Real" World

Of course, believing in the Meditator's worldview doesn't mean that you won't spend a lot of your day to day life in the Westerner's world. And, that being the case, it's convenient, even necessary to act as if cause and effect, life and death, good and evil, were real, and meaningful.

A theoretical physicist knows that his kitchen table is composed largely of the empty space between electrons. However, he confidently uses it to support his lunch. An Australian Aborigine believes in "dream time," a mystical reality in which dreams and spirits rule the earth, determining the outcome of all events. Yet he also depends on his knowledge of animal behavior and local geography in order to live.

You can live, and act, in the world using the Westerner's view. At the same time, you can begin to open your mind to the possibility that the Meditator's worldview has a validity of its own. The following section may help you to accept the Meditator's view (on an intellectual level, at least) right now.

Why We Might as Well Believe

As you continue to meditate, the Meditator's worldview will begin to feel more right to you on a gut, or emotional level. But today, you probably feel doubtful about it, and wonder: Can the Meditator's worldview possibly be real?

My answer to that is practical, rather than scientific or spiritual. And this same answer also works for what is perhaps humankind's oldest question: "Is there life after death?"

There seems to be a certain amount of evidence that some part of a person may persist after the body dies, although it's impossible to know for sure, until you die yourself. But I am sure, dead sure, that we just can't lose by maintaining a belief in continuing existence after the death of the body. "How can this be?" you may well ask. I'll tell you.

If we're right, we'll be prepared for our continued existence. And throughout this present life, we'll have had the faith and support that comes from a belief in undying consciousness.

If we're wrong, and absolute nothingness follows death, we'll never realize our mistake. But we'll still have gained the same benefits from that belief during our life! It's a bet that we really can't lose!

On the other hand, let's say that we may choose to disbelieve in consciousness after death. However, if we're right, and nothingness follows death, we'll never have the satisfaction of knowing that we were right. And if we're wrong, not only will we be unprepared for whatever comes next, but we'll have cheated ourselves out of the benefits of belief in some type of life after death during this lifetime! What a lousy deal!

I feel exactly the same way about the Meditator's worldview. If I'm wrong in my belief, I'll never know. And right or not, my trust in the Meditator's worldview can help me to live my life now with increased acceptance and confidence!

Enlightenment: What Is It?

In my opinion, enlightenment refers to the mental state in which the mind has become clear enough to embrace the Meditator's worldview, at least most of the time. That is, to comprehend that everything is connected to everything else, and physical reality is not the whole truth by a long shot. To understand that the body is an expression of an underlying consciousness, rather than consciousness being merely a biochemical by-product of the body. And to live by such knowledge, with one's mind unclouded by the confusing fears and desires of daily life.

As you may already have guessed, enlightenment isn't an especially easy place to get to. If it were, we'd all be walking around enlightenedly, there'd be no more crime, poverty, hatred, or war, and I'd have to go back to writing harmonica books!

Don't spend too much time now worrying about how "successful" you will be in attaining enlightenment. Forget about asking "Am I there yet?" As the old cliché says (and most clichés are backed by more than a grain of the truth or they would never have made it to clichéhood): "It's the journey, not the destination, that counts." On the road to enlightenment, getting there is much more than half the fun! It's most of the work, as well! And, to quote another old chestnut, "Even the longest journey begins with but a single step." A single Three Minute Meditation may be only a small step, but it will start you on your way, if you'll only try it. Go back to page 21 and try the Breath-Counting Meditation before reading on.

Steps on the Road

The steps described on the next page are all elements of the journey towards mental self-control and that elusive state of enlightenment. Each step corresponds to a series of Three Minute Meditation exercises in Part Two of this book. Reading about these steps will help you to understand why the exercises are important. But of course, doing the exercises is really the important part!

It wasn't easy to put these steps into any logical order. As you'd expect after reading about the Meditator's worldview, they melt, blend, and overlap into each other. But I am certain that for most people, Step One, Clearing the Mind, is the place to begin. In fact, you could easily spend an entire lifetime—or three—just on Step One! I still spend about 80 or 90 percent of my meditation time with the mind-clearing exercises.

Step Two, Watching the Mind, seems to follow naturally after Clearing the Mind, and Step Three, Taming the Mind, follows after that. But please feel free to try any of the Three Minute Meditations, in any order, that appeal to you, once you've begun to use the mind-clearers.

Of the Mind-tamers, the idea of compassion especially is crucial. Without compassion, even learning to meditate becomes just another opportunity to judge yourself harshly.

The First Step: Clearing the Mind

Almost all of the benefits of meditation can be obtained from practicing just the Clearing the Mind Meditations! Each of these exercises helps to quiet the constant, ongoing stream of chatter in the mind.

Feeling overwhelmed by theoretical speculations? Then go to page 71 right now, directly to the Clearing the Mind Meditations.

The Second Step: Watching the Mind

The exercises related to Step Two will help you observe the thoughts that flow through your mind. Instead of becoming involved in the specific content of each thought, you'll begin to see the process by which thoughts arise and pass away. And once you learn to watch that ongoing "movie" in your mind, just like a film or TV show, you'll also learn to be able to "get up and leave" or "change channels" whenever you choose to do so!

The Third Step: Taming the Mind

The Mind-tamers are four key concepts—"Compassion," "Visualization," "Relaxation," and the "Don't Know"—that will help you work with all of the Three Minute Meditation Exercises.

How Long Should It Take?

Don't be discouraged if these steps sound difficult. Nobody expects you to master them in a hurry. In fact, the Buddha said that enlightenment takes, on the average, 100,000 mahacalpas. And one mahacalpa is approximately the time it would take for a bird, dragging a silk scarf from its beak over the top of Mount Everest once a year, to wear the mountain down to sea level. So don't worry about finishing your quick sprint to enlightenment, but realize instead that you'd better start right now!

On Clearing the Mind

Minds are just chock-full of thoughts. You may sometimes be able to concentrate so intensely on a specific task that no distracting thoughts interfere—for a while. But soon enough a moment of restlessness, or doubt, or desire, or fear creeps in. And, thoughts being what they are, when your mind isn't strongly focused—when you're driving, or eating, or just relaxing by yourself—your mind may jump from thought to thought like the proverbial "drunken monkey" leaps aimlessly from branch to branch.

Most of the time, our mental attention is directed outwards, to other people, to the outside world. Our mind is full of thoughts that plan for the future, or analyze the past. We constantly make judgments about everything that passes into our mental field of view: I like this person, dislike that one she's beautiful, he's a jerk. And some thoughts may last a lifetime, as when we spend years being obsessed by the same strong desire, or beating ourselves endlessly with the same seemingly "unmanageable" fears.

On Watching the Mind

When a thought enters your mind, do you feel obligated to pay attention to it? Perhaps you can simply brush some thoughts aside. Other thoughts, especially fears and desires, seem to expand to fill your entire awareness, although you may consciously want to be rid of them. Often it may seem as though you have little control over your thoughts, especially when an unpleasant image or unacceptable desire occurs again and again despite your conscious wish to be rid of it.

We'll learn to work with thoughts by noticing them, counting them, labeling them. Soon we'll begin to recognize familiar patterns and sequences of thoughts.

Instead of only paying attention to the specific content of each thought, we'll begin to see the process by which thoughts arise and pass away. As we better understand this process through watching the mind, we'll become able to choose how to deal with each

When we work with the Clearing the Mind Meditations, we simply focus our attention onto just one thing, whether it's our breath, our walking, a candle flame, or whatever. While concentrating our attention onto the chosen object of our meditation, we try not to be distracted by those same thoughts that harass us normally. They will inevitably sneak in, and that's okay. But even a few seconds of mental clarity can feel really soothing.

This practice of keeping the mind clear by consciously focusing the attention is a wonderful exercise in mental control. And as the mind clears, we can move on to the next step, Watching the Mind.

thought that arises. We'll pay attention to the ones we want to pay attention to, and gently withdraw attention from those that we don't want to pay attention to. Eventually we'll be controlling our thoughts, rather than being controlled by them.

After we've practiced the Clearing the Mind exercises, we'll find it becoming easier to observe our own thoughts, as though they actually were scenes on a movie screen. Our increasing ability to consciously focus our attention becomes a powerful tool, like a searchlight that we can aim at the dark corners of our own minds. This is Watching the Mind.

And our thoughts will control us, if we allow them to. As Epictetus said, more than 2,000 years ago, "Men are not worried by things that happen, but by their thoughts about those things."

No one can control the things that happen in the world. We are all at the mercy of the virus, the accident, the natural disaster, the aging process. But we can control our mental reactions to whatever happens, if we just learn to understand how our thought process works.

At the Movies

I would like to take the movie analogy a bit further now. Please consider these two distinctly different ways of being part of the audience at a film:

If we choose, we can focus our attention very narrowly on the theater's screen, and watch just the *content* of the film that is playing. When watching in this way, if sad events occur on the screen, we will feel sad. If happy events occur, we'll feel happy. If the filmmakers are skillful propagandists, it will be simple for them to manipulate our beliefs and feelings. For instance, the German movie *Das Boot* (The Boat), about a German submarine crew struggling for life, was upsetting to many audiences in this country because it virtually forced them to root for the Nazi submariners.

Alternatively, we can focus our conscious attention more widely on the entire process of being at the movies. Then we will be aware not only of the action on the screen, but also of the fact that it is "just" a movie. So, as we watch the film, we will also be conscious of many other aspects of the situation. Is the theater crowded or empty? Are the other patrons engrossed or bored? What special effects or techniques were used to produce the scene that's playing right now? What feelings does each scene or character evoke for us? Do we like or dislike having those feelings? What were the goals of the director and the producer of the movie?

We can relate to our own minds in these same two ways. The type of thinking that most of us do, most of the time, is *content* thinking. We become engrossed in each passing thought. Is that a fearful thought arising? We become anxious. Is that a thought about loneliness? We feel lonely. If two conflicting thoughts happen to arise at the same time, like a dessert-desire thought and a fat-anxiety thought, we feel confused. We are so involved in the content of each thought that comes through our mind that perhaps it seems that we actually are nothing but the sum, the total, of our thoughts.

Relating to Your Mind Rather than Reacting to Your Thoughts

But when we learn to look at the process of our thinking, to watch our thoughts, we realize that they are not us, any more than a rock, or a book, or anything else that we can see outside of ourselves is us. And we can begin, as Stephen Levine says, to "relate to our mind, instead of from it." Or, as the most modern of neuropsychologists might say, we can begin to "let the orbitofrontal cortex [the part of the brain that analyzes and adjusts an emotional reaction *during* that reaction] override the limbic system [the primitive part of the brain that launches the fight-or-flight response]."

Relating to your mind means mentally "stepping back" to watch exactly what your mind is doing, without getting hung up in the content of any particular thought. It means being able to notice a fearful thought and say, "Ahh, there's a fearful thought," without automatically reacting by becoming fearful. It means being able to notice a lustful thought and say, "Uh-huh, there's a lustful thought," without automatically reacting by becoming consumed with desire and/or guilt. When we learn how to relate to our mind, we can choose how to react to any thought, instead of having our old habitual or automatic reaction to that thought. I'll talk more about this in the section on fears and phobias, in Part Three.

As we learn to watch our thoughts, we begin to see habitual thought patterns, or habitual reactions to thoughts, that are particularly our own. For some of us, tiredness will always cause fearful thoughts to arise. For one person, the sight of an expensive car may result in angry thoughts ("Rich jerk! He doesn't deserve a car like that!"), or for another, result in greedy thoughts ("When I have money, I'll have a car like that, plus a yacht!"). The sight of someone doing better than we are may lead to self-hating thoughts that could express themselves in ways as varied as hypochondria or despair. Or it might produce an envious thought. And that envious thought might then bring up a guilty thought, and so on . . .

Got time for a quick breath count (page 21)?

Sneezing Your Way to Enlightenment

I used to believe that a sneeze was something that "just happened." Unless I had caught a cold, or got pepper or dust up my nose, a sneeze usually seemed to come out of nowhere, and to be nearly unavoidable. Occasionally, of course, I'd notice a "pre-sneeze tickle" in my nose, and then I'd be able to delay or even prevent the actual "ah-choo," if I chose to struggle with it.

After some practice with the various breath meditations described in this book, I often find myself able to observe the entire sneeze process with greater clarity. Instead of noticing the ticklish feeling just seconds before it blossoms forth into a full-fledged sneeze, I now begin to note a tiny sensation of pressure or heat at the back of my nose, long before it becomes uncomfortable enough to motivate even a sniff or nose-wrinkle. I then focus my attention on the sensation itself, without labeling it as a nuisance, without wondering whether I'll have to sneeze or not. Just sensation: Is it hot or cold, steady or flickering? Where exactly is it located, way back towards the sinus or nearer the tip of the nose?

Surprisingly, the urge to sneeze almost always disappears when treated in this manner. The nose-tickle dwindles into nothingness, and I turn the focus of my attention back to my breathing. Most sensations and thoughts can be effectively dealt with in exactly the same way. Observing them closely gives us a great deal of power to control our reactions to them.

Taming My "Rambo Mind"

I used to be troubled by "macho" thoughts. For no apparent reason (but usually while walking the streets of the city at night) I'd find myself having "Rambo"-type fantasies of being powerful, tough, even dangerous. I enjoyed these thoughts to some extent, but they also frightened me and seemed inappropriate.

Once I began to observe my own mind with closer attention, I could see that these macho thoughts weren't unavoidable, didn't just "come out of nowhere." Instead, they were always preceded by a fleeting sensation of fear and vulnerability which triggered the Rambo thoughts, just as the sneeze was always preceded by a nose-tickle.

I'm now able to recognize these Rambo thoughts as my mind's attempts to avoid frightened feelings of being powerless. With this new awareness, I can acknowledge, accept, and then soothe my fearful thoughts with compassion whenever they arise. I deal directly with them, and no longer have to react in the old way of trying to cover them up with macho mindgames!

The Wild and Crazy Mind

Imagine thinking that you were the only person in the world who needed to urinate every day. You'd be acutely aware that you must continually perform this dirty, "unnatural" act, but you might never see anyone else do it. Einstein pee? Robert Redford take a leak? Impossible!

> It's really important to realize that everybody has a wild and crazy mind, filled with the same type of untamed, tangled thoughts that run through your own mind.

It's just as painful, if slightly less ridiculous, not to realize that everybody has the same kind of drunken-monkey mind as you do. Few people are open enough to talk to you about the fears, phobias, and fantasies in their minds. So your own mind is really the only one whose swirling multitude of strange thoughts you can easily be aware of. But knowing that we're all in roughly the same mental boat helps me to take my own bizarre ruminations just a bit less personally.

Letting Go of Thoughts

I began to understand the need to take thoughts (especially repetitive and self-hating thoughts) less personally, and also the need to let go of such negative thoughts as quickly as possible, when I worked at the Haight Ashbury Free Clinic in San Francisco. I often had the job of "talking down" a person brought in on a bad acid trip. I soon realized that most acid "freakouts" were caused by a person's inability to let go of a disturbing thought.

John was a frequent visitor to the clinic. He would come in high on LSD, hallucinating, for instance, that his dead grandmother was crawling up his leg, a knife clenched between her teeth. He'd read of that image somewhere, and it "just stuck in his mind." So he'd "see" grandma, and then think, "Wow! That's a crazy thought." And next, "I must be crazy to even have a thought like that . . . is she still there?" Half an hour of this, and he'd end up at the Haight Clinic, talking to me!

In contrast, the Paisley Lady was a street person who would rarely come to the clinic, except to say hello. She once told me about her method for dealing with potential bad trips—that is, trips in which she would have the same weird thought repeatedly. "Like there's an army of mice, and they're covering the floor. And they're all coming at me wearing little tiny uniforms, with a mouse general in front . . . " She too would say, "Wow, that's a crazy thought." Then she'd laugh, and let her mind go on to the next wild thought, or focus on the patterns made by the hallucinatory mice or the sun on the floor, or her own toes! She'd had plenty of experience with weird thoughts, and was good at letting go of them from one moment to the next!

Living in the Now

Some memory-thoughts and some planning-thoughts are useful, or at least necessary, for functioning in this or any culture. But it's important to remember that when we focus our attention on a thought of the past or a thought of the future, we are bringing past or future into our present, thus pushing the actual present, the "now," out of mind.

Most people who meditate find that they don't have to do nearly as much "future planning" or "past remembering" as they once thought they did. A healthy, well-cared-for body can react quickly and naturally to the immediate physical requirements of any situation, whether they involve fighting or fleeing, sleeping deeply or remaining awake and alert. Likewise, a mind cleared by meditation tends to respond naturally and appropriately to the mental circumstances of the present moment, whatever those circumstances may be.

When we're thinking of how much work we have to do while our boss is talking to us, or thinking of what we'll say next during a conversation with a friend, we can't be present to listen and to respond meaningfully right now. Similarly, when we're busy filling our fork for the next bite while chewing the present mouthful, or pondering dessert during the entrée, we're simply not present to enjoy our eating right now.

I began to understand this as I learned to improvise on the blues harmonica. Worrying about the note I had just played or planning ahead for the sequence that I wanted to play next impaired my ability to create improvisations freely. I had to learn to let go of a note as soon as I had played it, without thinking about the note to come. Only then did my music begin to improve.

The Chatterbox Mind

Often, we are not even completely aware of all of our thoughts. Many of us suffer from an internal monologue that runs intermittently, a critical, judgmental, internal voice that seems to love to offer gratuitous and usually negative comments. These comments slink through our mind half-noticed, and, like small leaks in the bottom of a large boat, often have a long-term or cumulative effect, which is not a pleasant one.

I used to use the first line or two of The Beatles song "I'm A Loser" to berate myself with. Anytime that I did anything that didn't work out perfectly, I'd subconsciously croon "I'm a looo-oo-ooser . . . " to myself, thus reinforcing my negative feelings.

Once I began to clear and to watch my mind through meditation, I was able to see what I was doing (at least sometimes), and began to let go of this self-hating habit. Before I started meditating I couldn't see it happening. I couldn't catch myself in the act, so I wasn't able to deal with this behavior.

I feel a lot better now that my mind is no longer singing that darn tune! You'll feel happier and more positive when you begin to quiet the chatter of your mind, too.

Four Techniques to Tame the Mind

These four techniques and their related exercises are powerful tools for calming and controlling the body and mind. They can be used alone or to add depth and power to any meditation.

Visualization

Visualization is the art of creating mental images. Since mental images can have a powerful effect on our bodies and minds, as discussed on page 10, practicing this skill will better allow us to use it to our advantage. Improved visualization skills will help us with all of the Three Minute Meditations, but most importantly with the Relaxation Meditation and with the crucial Master Skill Visualization Exercise, which is the last one in the book. Don't miss it!

Everyone can picture an elephant, a rabbit, or a Volkswagen in their mind's eye. Most of us can produce a clear enough mental image of our own neighborhood to describe the houses or buildings next to our own. It is reported that inventor Nicola Tesla could visualize a new engine in his mind, allow it to "run" for a few hours, and then "see" which parts showed wear or metal fatigue! He was one serious visualizer!

Relaxation

Relaxation is to the body what meditation is to the mind: a process of turning the attention inward while letting go of the physical tensions that normally inhabit our bodies. We'll learn to use visualization to help us relax, and learn to use relaxation to help us meditate.

Compassion

Probably the most important meditation we can do is just to spend time with ourselves in a state of compassion and forgiveness. It sounds easy, it even sounds simplistic, but it works. And until we can forgive and feel compassion for ourselves, we can't truly offer it to anyone else.

In this high-pressure, performance-oriented society, we often judge ourselves and find ourselves lacking. We're not as beautiful as the movie stars, as rich as the stock speculators, as wise as the scientists that we constantly see in the news.

Thus, the art of compassion will aid us also in those meditations involving both judgment and investigation of the truth. And,

---

We monitor, we judge, we boss ourselves mercilessly—as though our mind were an administrator, seeking to constantly improve some personal bottom line. But when compassion becomes our guideline, even for a moment, we learn instead to investigate ourselves as an anthropologist studies a foreign culture. Alert curiosity replaces disdain or denial, the usual attempts to avoid pain by closing off the heart.

Stepping away from a place of critical judgment, we can seek to find out what is true, even if it's not flattering. Then we can bring compassion to these "rough spots." It's easy to love our finer points and nobler qualities, but the unflattering aspects of ourselves—our fears, greeds, stupidities—are exactly the parts that we most need to be compassionate towards!

as I've said before, an awareness of compassion will prevent us from letting meditation become just another race to lose, just another way to be hard on ourselves.

Applying Compassion to Thoughts

For me, frustration often leads to anger. When business dealings, relationships, or other events don't go the way I want them to, I first feel frustrated, then threatened by my own lack of control. Almost instantaneously the feelings of frustration and fear turn into anger, as my mind attempts to cover up these insecure and painful feelings with more aggressive ones. Acting upon these aggressive feelings, I may then lash out at myself, or at loved ones, without even knowing why.

But when I can recognize the initial frustration and fearful feelings as they arise, I can meet them with compassion. A moment of Compassion Meditation (page 104) will often break the chain of frustration-to-fear-to-anger, and allow me to face the frustration and fear directly. It's not easy to face up to my own inability to control people, events, and things. But I'd rather directly face these feelings and the pain that they bring, than encounter the far greater pain of the misdirected anger, with its warlike attack on myself or others.

Even if I do get angry, I may be able, after a moment, to remember to be compassionate towards myself, both for my pain, and for having become mad. All humans feel anger and must somehow learn to deal with this emotion. Feeling compassion for my anger is far more healing in the long run than feeling guilt for my anger, or feeling angry at myself for my anger. Feeling compassion for myself allows me to "watch the movie" in my mind and step outside my old knee-jerk reaction of pain, anger, and self-hate.

"Don't Know"

Although no one likes a know-it-all, we're often hesitant to admit (a word that expresses our reluctance and resistance) that we "don't know." We usually think that if we don't know the answer, or don't know what's going on, then we'd darned well better be trying to find out!

Yet there can be an openness and a satisfaction to the "don't know" state. There's room for anything in the openness of "don't know"—it leaves us space for every possibility. "Don't know" is at the heart of Zen Buddhism's "beginner's mind," the Jain's "doctrine of maybe" and the Christian injunction to "be as a small child."

Adding compassion to "don't know" gives us a wry acknowledgment of the uncertainty of living in this imperfect and frustrating world. So much of what goes on in our lives is impossible to predict, or control. Learning to cultivate a sense of don't know, learning to let this uncertainty be okay, helps us recognize and accept the painful truth—that we are often unable to control what happens in our lives, to ourselves, to our loved ones. Once we accept this fact, we no longer have to waste energy denying it.

Exit Part One

You now have more than enough theoretical knowledge to begin meditating. It's time to start doing some of the exercises in Part Two, especially if you haven't already been practicing the breathing meditation on page 21.

PART II

The Exercises

Welcome to Part Two of *The Three Minute Meditator*. I'll begin by talking about gurus. Then I'll discuss my original, if slightly unconventional, concept of "MetaPhysical Fitness," and tell you how Three Minute Meditations can help keep you in tip-top "spiritual shape"! After that come the Three Minute Meditation Exercises themselves, the "hows," or "nuts and bolts," of meditation.

These exercises are divided into groups, and I'll explain the "whys" of each group in an introductory section. Once again, especially important paragraphs will be boxed. If you'd like more information on any of the first three groups: Clearing the Mind, Watching the Mind, and Taming the Mind, go back and read Part One, unless you've already done so. The bibliography will direct you to a few of my favorite books on some of these and other categories of meditation, as well.

But remember, *doing* these exercises is more important than reading about them. So feel free, if you like, to read only the boxed paragraphs, and scan the section titles. Then spend a couple of days or weeks doing the first few Three Minute Meditations that follow, before you read the rest of the text.

Two Troubles with Gurus

Gurus: Not a Prerequisite

I am beginning Part Two with a discussion of gurus, because many people think that you *need* one in order to meditate or to become enlightened. And that's the first trouble with gurus.

A guru is what you might end up with if you crossed a coach or a trainer with a priest or a rabbi—basically, someone who coaches your spiritual development. Of course, the best coach in the world won't help you at all if you don't want to exercise or practice your chosen sport. And the saintliest priest won't help you to be religious, unless you decide to work at it yourself as well.

Without the desire to work at meditating, having a guru is mostly a spiritual status symbol, a way to appear as though you were following a spiritual path without having to pay the price of hard, mental work. If a would-be meditator indeed has the desire

Learning to meditate is an "inside job." Although a guru may provide a good role model for the beginning meditator, it is the disciple him- or herself who must do the actual meditation.

to do the work, he or she will be able to proceed along the meditative road quite well, with or without the benefit of a guru!

For these reasons, I believe that it can't hurt to begin meditating without a guru. Once you have some "basic" meditation hours under your headband, you'll be much better prepared to choose to follow any particular meditative discipline (or guru) that appeals to you.

> Perhaps, like me, you'll decide to enjoy and respect the many fine gurus and other teachers whose lectures, writings, and retreats are available, without joining any one group or sect to the exclusion of the rest.

Practice Makes Perfect

The second main trouble with gurus is that so many of them seem to have embarrassingly worldly vices, like sleeping with their disciples, alcoholism, engaging in power struggles, or collecting expensive toys, most notably Rolls-Royces. Although the point may be made that some gurus like to teach by negative example (the old "do as I say, not as I do" routine), I believe that there is a simpler explanation for these often highly publicized lapses in guru deportment.

My theory is that we must learn to differentiate between the *teaching guru* and the *practicing guru.*

Let's think about doctors for a moment. Picture the best-teaching doc in the world—urbane, comfortable, and articulate in front of an entire amphitheater of overworked and stressed-out medical students. This knowledgeable physician may not be capable of doing nearly as good a job of stitching you up after a minor auto accident as some underpaid intern in a busy urban emergency room. In short, the realm of *teaching* expertise does not necessarily translate into the realm of *doing* expertise. The med-school doc is a *teaching* doctor, not a *practicing* doctor.

In the music world, it's well known that a great teacher is not often an exceptional player, and vice versa. I'm a world-class harmonica *teacher,* and can sound great at any gig—for half an hour. But there are hundreds of guys who could blow me away in an all-night jam session. Why is that? Because I practice *teaching* plenty, but I just don't practice *playing* enough. I'm not a *practicing* musician . . .

We see two themes emerging. First, it requires different skills to *teach* than it does to *do*. The most highly visible gurus in this country are usually teaching gurus. They are by turns flamboyant, mysterious, and eccentric. Although they are often very good at telling *you* how to "become enlightened," their own personal lives may not be as exemplary as we would wish.

In contrast, most practicing gurus are reclusive, unassuming types, more concerned with the depth of their own meditations than with their popularity ratings. In fact, by all accounts, one of the things that most strikes the person encountering the practicing guru, like Suzuki Roshi or Sri Nisargadatta, is the guru's "utter ordinariness." But of course "ordinariness" doesn't play too well on the prime-time television shows, so that although practicing gurus sometimes teach, they often are not well known.

Our second, and more important theme has to do with practice. Musicians practice, athletes practice, doctors practice. But full-time, serious teachers rarely have time to practice enough. Neither do many of the teaching gurus, which is why their lives do not always display the beneficial effects of meditation!

Imagine the pressures and temptations placed on a guru, especially one coming to this country from a sexually constrained, materially poor culture. It's no wonder that so many become distracted from their meditation practices! (Our own homegrown, USA gurus are often easily distracted, too, with even less excuse.) And once even gurus stop their practice of meditation, they're subject to all the usual human desires and fears, with lots of money and power to indulge themselves! Since we live in a culture that loves to dethrone heroes and wise men, both with and without good cause, the next stop is prime billing on the evening-news exposé!

All kidding aside, this section has not been merely an exercise in the time-honored art of guru-knocking, although it's always fun to lambaste those who fail to practice what they preach. But as we'll see in the next section, practice is truly at the heart of meditation.

MetaPhysical Fitness

It's often tempting to think in terms of specific, concrete "things" rather than in terms of ongoing "processes." And it would be so convenient if "enlightenment" were a thing, that we could obtain or achieve once and keep forever, like a rowing machine or a law degree. But it's not. It's an ongoing process and it requires ongoing practice. It's rather like getting (and staying) in shape.

Getting in shape isn't too hard. A few weeks or months of weight lifting combined with the Scarsdale Diet and we look and feel great! Jogging and the Pritikin Diet will work also, or aerobic parachuting and the Rutabaga Diet. But just a few months of indolence and overindulgence, and we're again ready to enter the Pillsbury Doughboy Look-Alike Contest. Of course, even sporadic and feeble attempts at getting into shape are better than none, although the long-term effects of such lackadaisical efforts may be almost imperceptible.

I really like the comparison of meditating, or even of enlightenment, with the idea of getting in shape. Like getting in shape, there are a great variety of equally effective ways to go about meditating. Like getting in shape, anyone can meditate, although it sometimes *seems* easier or more natural for certain people than for others. (Usually someone other than ourselves.)

Once a person has become physically fit, everything
they do both reflects their fitness and helps to increase
it. They walk with bounce and balance, and climb stairs
instead of taking elevators. Once a person begins to
meditate, everything that happens to them presents a
great opportunity to both demonstrate and to improve
their meditative skills. Fears and desires, annoyances
and disappointments, all become grist for the meditative mill!

Unfortunately, just as with getting in shape, if we stop meditating, we lose its benefits. This, as discussed in a previous section, may be what happens to so many of the famous teaching gurus.

Finally, like getting in shape, we have to begin meditating somewhere. Very old or infirm persons wouldn't start their exercise programs by trying to run the Boston Marathon, but might instead begin with daily walks around the block. A modest beginning, but certainly steps in the right direction!

Someone new to meditation, or someone lacking time and commitment to a meditative practice, surely wouldn't buy a one-way ticket to India. Even twenty minutes twice a day at home might be more than they could do at first. But a few of the following Three Minute Meditations might be just what the (meta)physician ordered!

Each of the Three Minute Meditations is an exercise for
the mind. Like exercises for the body, they must be first
practiced under controlled conditions in order to later
obtain the benefits that they can provide in "real life"
situations.

Martial Arts of the Mind

The karate student practices in the "dojo," or karate studio. He or she first practices a variety of punches and kicks, doing each one separately, carefully, repeating each movement tens of thousands of times. After mastering each move in isolation, the student begins to practice more complicated combinations of blows, performing each sequence hundreds or thousands of times. He or she then spars with other students or instructors. Finally, if one day these martial skills are needed on the street, in a real combat situation, this practice has fully prepared the student to use them.

Similarly, whitewater kayakers must learn a technique known as the "eskimo roll," which enables them to turn their kayak right-side-up after it has turned bottom-up in a river rapid. They first learn this technique in a swimming pool. Once they feel comfortable "rolling" in the pool, they go out and purposely capsize their boat in a very small rapid, and then try to roll. Gradually, they progress on to roll practice in larger and more dangerous rapids, until they can confidently roll *anywhere* on the river.

You'll begin by practicing a simple type of Three Minute Meditation called the Clearing the Mind exercises. At first, you'll try to do them in calm surroundings, devoting at least a full three minutes to each one. After you learn to gain a moment or two of mental clarity at a time, you'll add another type of meditation, called the Watching the Mind exercises. Again, you'll initially practice these exercises under conditions of relative comfort, so that later on you'll be able to perform them skillfully under stressful circumstances.

Once you become familiar with the mind-watching exercises, you'll begin to use your new knowledge to increase mind control in "real-life" situations, starting with practice during easy, non-threatening events. Instead of getting anxious or angry, you'll just *watch* your thoughts as the omelet arrives slightly overdone, or as the elevator refuses to stop at your floor. This practice will improve both the quality of your life, and the quality of your meditation!

As you gain practice and confidence, you'll be able to apply your meditative skills to more serious mental and interpersonal predicaments. Having the ability to calmly and confidently deal with *whatever* comes into our lives is truly the "Master Skill"!

More About Meditation

For most nonmeditators, the above sort of experience just occurs spontaneously, without planning. When it happens, it happens. However, meditators *make* these meditations happen, because we understand the great value of clearing, focusing, and controlling the mind. We do this by using various time-honored mind-clearing techniques. Some of these will seem strange or unusual at first, but you'll get used to them.

Other meditations that you'll be practicing won't involve doing anything that you don't normally do. Only your attitude will change, as you consciously try to focus your attention on whatever is happening, whether that's brushing your teeth or washing dishes. Instead of planning for the day, or wishing that the gravy on the bottom of the pot wasn't burnt on quite so solidly, you will make the brushing, or the washing, into a meditation—just by focusing exclusively on it. No future planning, no past memories: just scrubbing, rinsing. This conscious focusing of attention is sometimes called "mindfulness." It is the most powerful tool that we possess, a mental spotlight that can illuminate any action or thought!

As I've said before, meditation is the art of mental self-control. Meditation is not anything occult, or esoteric, or "outside" of normal, daily, life.

In fact, you probably do a certain type of meditation already, even if you don't call it that. Whenever you keep your attention so strongly focused on something that no other thoughts intrude, that's a form of Clearing the Mind meditation. Watching the waves break on the beach or staring into the flames of a campfire can be meditation (albeit a short one, for most of us, before thoughts intrude). Hang gliding is a meditation for some, harmonica playing for others. Anything that forces all of your awareness onto just one thing, so that the usual chatter of the mind is momentarily stilled. No fear or desire thoughts about the future, or "could of, would of, should of" thoughts about the past.

Anything done with focus, awareness, or mindfulness is a meditation, and will eventually take us in the direction of enlightenment, no matter how mundane (dishwashing enlightenment? toothbrushing enlightenment?) it may seem. Once we've learned to meditate, to be mindful—every action and every thought can become the momentary focus of a meditation.

What Is a Three Minute Meditation?

Each Three Minute Meditation is a specific exercise to help us gain mental self-control. Each one helps us to focus our mental attention, to become mindful.

The Three Minute Meditation program is unique. Most other meditation methods advise that you set aside a certain time or times each day for meditation. Some demand that a shrine of some sort be built, and that meditation only take place there. The most extreme programs require you to live in a monastery, far from the distractions of the world.

But limiting meditation to specific times or places can have two negative consequences. First, such demands can be hard to adhere to, especially for the beginning meditator who has not yet felt the positive results of a daily meditative practice and thus is not yet heavily committed to it. Second, a time-and-place-specific meditation program somehow sets meditation aside from "normal" existence. Practicing the Three Minute Meditation way avoids both of these problems, although, of course, once you begin meditating, you can then explore and pursue *any* style of practice that appeals to *you*.

It's obviously easier to find time to do a number of short meditations during a day than to set aside one or two chunks of twenty or thirty minutes every day. Many of the Three Minute Meditations can be done while walking, or eating, or even stopped at a red light. Others can be practiced during a quick visit to the bathroom!

Once you get the hang of Three Minute Meditating, you'll find yourself doing many "mini-meditations" that will be amazingly effective in calming or centering you—even though they only take a few seconds! You'll also probably find yourself wanting to do some longer meditations, of ten or twenty minutes or more. I like to do at least one longer one, most mornings.

I, and many others, find that integrating our meditation practice throughout the day helps us to use meditation skills in daily life. Ideally, meditation becomes a way of life, a way of relating to the world, rather than something that you do for a little while every day.

Every year or so, I try to attend a ten-day retreat in the Vipassana monastic tradition. No talking, no eye contact, no reading or writing. Approximately sixteen hours a day of alternating walking and breathing meditation, with eating meditations strongly advised during mealtimes. They feel great, and I get very high and clear. But then they're over, and I have to come home!

Long retreats, and esoteric disciplines, can be of great value— monastic traditions exist in nearly every culture. But sooner or later, unless you're a monk, you'll have to come home—that is, you'll have to make your experience apply to daily life. With Three Minute Meditation, you're already home.

Question: What's the difference between a monk and a Three Minute Meditator?

Answer: Monks live in order to meditate better, and Three Minute Meditators meditate in order to live better.

How to Use These Exercises

The bottom line is this: Just try to do 'em! Memorizing every metaphysical word in this or any other book is worth less to you than spending three diligent minutes with the simplest of the exercises that follow.

Although many beginners may want to start out with the easiest Clearing the Mind exercises (the first five), remember that there is a lot of overlap between the groups of meditations. For example, mind clearing will help you to Watch the Mind, and to Live in the Now. Mind watching is an essential part of doing the Judging and Compassion exercises. Pushing limits is really a part of every exercise, and so on. So, since the exercises are interconnected, when you practice one, you are actually doing many. And thus trying them *all* may actually help you to do the ones you decide to concentrate on. But for some people, trying them all may seem like an overwhelming amount to do right at first.

I'll now present two strategies that you can follow in deciding which of the exercises to use. I'll describe each strategy, and you can determine which one feels most right to you, and then begin to use it.

Whichever strategy you pick, please make sure to read about, and practice, the exercise called the "Master Skill" on page 130. It will help you to do any of the others.

The "Crawl Before You Walk" Approach

You don't have to do anything fancy to get results, as this tale indicates.

The story goes that an early Catholic bishop went to visit three old monks who lived on an island, because he'd heard that they believed in Jesus, and he wanted to teach them to pray in the proper manner. When he arrived, he discovered that their only prayer or meditation (referring to the Christian idea of the Trinity) was the simple "The Lord is Three, and we are three," repeated continuously.

The bishop spent days teaching the old men how to pray properly with long, complex Latin prayers and invocations. Then he and his entourage sailed away, satisfied with a job well done.

You can begin by choosing one of the two easiest mind clearing meditations, the Breath-Counting or the Walking Breath Exercises. These are easy because they are quite cut and dried, almost mechanical. If you follow the simple instructions, you cannot go wrong. They are the "meat and potatoes" of meditation, and I enjoy doing both at least a few times each day. Practice these for as long as you like. **If you did nothing but these two exercises daily, you would still derive great calmness and energy from your practice.**

But when his boat was only a few miles away from the island, the ship's lookout spied a mysterious blur overtaking them. It soon turned out to be the three monks, running over the surface of the water to catch the ship.

"Your Holiness," they panted as they came within shouting distance, "We've forgotten our new prayers!"

And the bishop was chastened, and bade them return to their former simple and effective practice.

If you prefer, you can spend just a few minutes doing the Breath-Counting and the Walking Breath exercises, maybe try the Chanting, Slow Walking, and Flame Meditations, and then read about all the rest, experimenting with any that particularly appeal to you. Find one that you like, and do it often throughout the day, or alternate between a few that interest you.

The Shotgun Approach

Psychologist and philosopher Ram Dass (Dr. Richard Alpert) recently stated (in the excellent video series, *How Then Shall We Live*, as mentioned on page 188) that he uses from 50 to 100 different meditation methods every day. He's a real Three Minute Meditator, even if he doesn't use that term!

Progressive Meditation: What's Easy and What's Hard

You're really the only person who can say what's easy or hard for you. In general, I've tried to arrange the exercises in the order of difficulty that meditators and teachers I know tend to agree on. But although there was some agreement that the first five exercises were the simplest, there was considerable disagreement about the ranking of the rest. So you'll just have to try them all for yourself!

There is a certain progression to the exercises. We start out by focusing the spotlight of our attention on the *counting* of natural processes, like breathing and walking. Then we proceed to focus attention on the *actual physical sensations* of walking, breathing, or other activities. We then begin to pay attention to our *thoughts* as they pass through our minds, by naming them, counting them, or judging them. Finally we focus attention directly upon *emotions* or *ideas* such as compassion, freedom, impermanence, or the elusive "I am."

What to Do When It Hurts

Sometimes, as we look deeply into ourselves, old or hidden pain can arise. It may not happen to you, but if it does, please be sure to read this section carefully.

If you are already under a doctor's or psychotherapist's care, you should definitely discuss this book with them before using it. By the way, psychotherapy and meditation make an especially effective combination! As you continue to meditate, previously unconscious material will come clearly into view, where it can be worked with.

If you are in great mental pain now, perhaps you should carefully read the entire book before doing any of the exercises, and then start out with the Compassion meditations. They are probably the most effective exercises in the book for dealing with suffering of any kind.

There are two distinct types of mental suffering. There's the suffering that occurs when we are not meditating, or before we've learned to meditate, when our thoughts, our fears and desires, cause us pain. This is the type of suffering that many of us experience on an *ongoing* basis. Since many nonmeditators have little control over their thoughts, this kind of suffering is hard to deal with. It may possibly diminish if we can change various circumstances in our lives. But it probably won't. Instead, the pain will merely change the new circumstances!

The type of suffering that may arise during meditation is different, although it can, on the surface, feel the same. But it is suffering whose purpose is to *end* further suffering. So if painful feelings arise while meditating, try to remember that these are the *temporary* pains that will help us to *end* the *ongoing* pain, just as the pain of the extraction is intended to end the ache of the infected tooth.

As long as we remember to use the mind-watching exercises to *observe* our pain, rather than just getting lost in the contents of the painful thoughts, we can *utilize* this *temporary* pain to reduce *ongoing* pain. I know, from personal experience, that this is a difficult concept to believe, especially when in a state of suffering. Using the Compassion exercise may be especially helpful, to ease the pain. It's what I try to do, when in pain, if I'm "together" enough to remember to do so.

When we learn about ourselves, we sometimes see elements of our personalities that we'd prefer to deny. If this happens to you, as it so often has to me, please read the section on compassion at the end of Part One (page 44), then go directly to the Compassion exercises following page 101.

General Instructions
for the Exercises

There are really only three important general instructions for doing the exercises.

The first is to remember that you are meditating, and that your attention is supposed to be focused on the object of meditation, be it your breath, your steps, your feet, a sound, or a candle. Whenever any other thought intrudes, *as soon as you notice* that you are no longer focused on the meditation, bring your attention back to the meditation.

The second is to be *compassionate.* Spending time berating yourself for not focusing on the meditation (because you momentarily thought of lunch, or work, or sex) is just more time spent not focusing on the meditation. No need to be critical—just go back to the meditation.

The third (which may help you with the second) is to realize that the thoughts which distract you from the meditation are actually *helping* you. They give you the opportunity to notice that you're no longer focused on the meditation, so that you can return your attention to it.

Think about trying to paper-train a puppy. It looks as though it has to pee. You place it on the newspaper. It wanders off. You gently, patiently bring it back. It wanders off again. *It is the act of being returned* to the newspaper that paper-trains the pup. If the foolish little thing never left the paper, you wouldn't have the opportunity to train it. So you don't kick it when it wanders off, nor give up in disgust. It's just the nature of a puppy to wander.

Likewise, it's the act of noticing the mind has wandered, and returning the attention to the meditation that helps us learn to focus the mind . . .

An Example

When I began to meditate, I was "plagued" by distracting thoughts. I'd try to focus on my breathing, but a typical meditation session might have gone something like this: "breathe in, breathe out . . . wow, I'm meditating . . . uh-oh, I'm not supposed to be thinking about meditating, I'm supposed to be focusing on my breathing . . . in, out . . . hungry . . . uh-oh . . . drat, I can't do this, I'm no good . . . in, out, in, out, in, out . . . hey, I've got it now! . . . feelings of pride . . . uh-oh, better go back to breathing . . . in, out, in out . . . wonder what's for lunch . . . darn . . . in, out, in, out . . . wonder if it's time to stop yet . . . and so on." Sometimes I'd get lost in a daydream of some sort, and my period of distraction would last for minutes at a time, far longer than I was ever able to concentrate on my breath!

Now that I'm more experienced, I still have plenty of sessions like that! But many times, I can just quickly notice that a thought has crept in, and go right back to my preferred business at hand, which is meditating. So a current session might look more like this: "breathe in, breathe out, in, out, in, out . . . ahh, a lunch thought . . . in, out, in, out . . . Doing Well! . . . ahh, that's a pride thought . . . in, out, in, out . . . ." Of course, sometimes I still spend more time being distracted, than being focused! But I notice the distractions more quickly, and return to the meditation!

On Diligence

It is important to be diligent in your attention to the meditation. That means that *as soon as you notice* that your attention has strayed from the meditation, you bring it gently but firmly back.

That means not spending even an extra second on that daydream, no matter how exciting it is (so forget the old "but wait—this is a really important thought I'm thinking—I'd better stick with it, and meditate later" trick). Don't waste even a second on self-critical thoughts like, "Darn it! There I go, thinking again." Simply *let go* of whatever thought it was that passed through, and come back to the meditation. Just for these three minutes, the meditation is your *preferred* thought—any others can wait.

It's a bit like training yourself to wear a seat belt. As soon as you notice that it isn't buckled, you put it on, *every time*, even if you're only three blocks away from your destination. Soon it becomes a habit (and a healthy one, at that).

On Body and Hand Position

Luckily for you, I don't require a full lotus position for meditation (can't do one, myself, without enriching my chiropractor)! I think that it's probably best to meditate (except for the walking-based meditations) while sitting up straight. Not ramrod rigid, but not slouching either, with your feet flat on the floor. Then again, you'll sometimes want to meditate while laying down, on the bus, in the bathroom, or standing in line. So don't worry much about body position. Sit up straight when it's convenient, and see if it makes any difference to your concentration.

However, for many people it is useful to maintain a particular and *consistent* hand position while doing most of their meditating. I favor having the thumb tip and forefinger tip of each hand very lightly touching, with the other fingers either curled or extended out.

Learning to maintain a standardized hand position can help to act as a "memory cue" or "trigger" for meditation. Once you get used to meditating, and begin to associate the hand position with meditating, just recreating the hand position will help you to enter into a meditative state of mind.

This can be especially useful in stressful situations, like a job interview, where you cannot take "time out" to go and meditate (unless you fake a bathroom break—a useful tactic at times). But simply touching thumb to forefinger while taking a deep and mindful breath can help to remind you of the peaceful place that you find in meditation, and give you energy to continue the interview with confidence. I'll amplify this concept in the section on "Relax Buttons" (page 166).

What to Do with Feelings of Doubt and Resistance

Minds being what they are, at some point yours is going to say to you: "This just won't work" or "Why bother?" And if you can learn to use the mind-watching exercises described later, you'll be able to use these thoughts as objects of focus for your attention. Just as smelly old manure can be turned into valuable fertilizer, you can use even thoughts of doubt and resistance to hone your meditation skills, merely by watching them. They will then become your teachers, instead of your tormentors.

Competitive Meditation

It's easy to get competitive, or goal-oriented, with meditation (or with anything else, in this high-pressure culture of ours). The late Tibetan guru Trungpa Rimpoche used to call this "Spiritual Materialism"!

Try to think of meditation as dance, rather than a race. In a race, the goal is to reach the end faster than anyone else, or faster than you've ever done it before. In a dance, the goal is to enjoy what you're doing while you're doing it. So try not to worry about whether your meditations are "improving," or about whether you're "doing it right." Just do it! Even in a race situation, excessive concern about how you are doing (looking back over your shoulder too much) will actually decrease your performance!

Clearing the Mind

Most of the following exercises operate on what I call the "distraction/subtraction" principle. By giving the mind a very simple but consuming set of instructions to follow, the "normal" mental monologue of fears, desires, memories and predictions can be stilled. The mind becomes just too busy to keep up its usual chatter.

After subtracting these above unwanted thoughts from the contents of the mind, you will gradually be able to directly observe the thought processes of the mind, with the mind-watching exercises. But for now, merely removing these "excess" thoughts from the mind will be your goal.

When asked how he could carve an elephant from an immense block of stone, the master sculptor replied: "I simply cut away everything that doesn't look like an elephant . . ." Carving away the excess thoughts from your mind will leave you with a clear and peaceful feeling, and eventually allow you to understand what really goes on in there!

> If not otherwise indicated, at first practice each
> meditation for three minutes, or longer if you prefer.
> Once you've learned the exercise, do it for as long or
> short as you like, from three seconds to three hours!

This first Three Minute Meditation involves our most basic need. We can live for days without water, weeks without food, and perhaps years without sex or a job. But one scant minute without breathing is a long time, for most of us. Yet how often do we really focus our attention exclusively on this most crucial of functions? Fortunately, for a person in good health, breathing doesn't take much thought—and we haven't usually given it much—until today.

Breath-Counting Meditation

Begin by practicing this meditation while sitting comfortably in a quiet place, with your hands in the thumb to forefinger position described on page 69. If you've already tried this exercise way back on page 21, well, do it again. As the old saying goes: "Don't just sit there—meditate!"

Simply *count* the exhale of each breath, mentally: "Inhale . . . one, Inhale . . . two, Inhale . . . three, Inhale . . . four" then begin again with "Inhale . . . one." Strive not to lose your count, and also try not to alter or regularize your breathing in any way. Try to feel the physical sensation of each breath, both inhale and exhale, as it passes through your nose or mouth.

If you find yourself thinking about *anything* except the feel of your breath and the number of that breath, return to focus on the sensation of breathing, and on the number of that breath. If you are not absolutely sure what number breath you're on, begin again with "In . . . one." No judging, no "I blew the count" thoughts, just back to "In . . . one."

Right now, consider the breath focus and count to be your "preferred" thoughts. Thoughts of lunch, memories, or other intruders will just be gently replaced by "In . . . one, In . . . two" and so on, *as soon as you notice them* creeping in. And they will! Of course it's difficult to stay focused! But with practice, it just gets easier and easier.

The beauty of this meditation is that, once learned, you can do it *anywhere*! Try it while waiting in line, or at the laundromat (no one can even tell that you're doing anything unusual)!

Experiment, if you like, with extending each count up to eight or ten. Is that easier or harder to do than a count of four? Want to be meditationally macho (or macha)? Every once in a while, see how many consecutive exhales you can count without losing yourself, and your count, in a thought. My personal record to date is 442, reached one competitive afternoon during a ten-day retreat.

Pride was my downfall: "Inhale . . . 439, Inhale . . . 440, Inhale . . . 441, Inhale . . . 442, Wow, I'm really doing great! I bet I've gotten further than anyone else here, me! David!—Uh oh, what number breath *was* that last one?—#%X@!!! . . . . . . Inhale . . . one, Inhale . . . two, Inhale . . . "

The Chore-Based Breath Count

Try this meditation after you've practiced at least a few sessions of the Breath-Counting Meditation. You'll be doing this one in conjunction with a specific task or chore that you do at least on a daily basis (preferably something short, and more or less mindless). For me, taking a short break to get a drink of water (average count, four breaths), putting paper into my computer printer (average count, six or seven breaths), or making popcorn in the microwave (average count, twenty breaths) work well.

I simply count the number of breaths it takes me to do the task (numbering each exhale, and without, of course, trying to control the speed or regularity of my respiration). Naturally, thoughts try to intrude, but for the duration of this particular task, my "job" is to get an accurate count of my breaths.

Some people seem to find this meditation slightly easier, or more compelling, than the more basic Breath-Counting Meditation. It has the added advantage of helping you integrate your meditation practice right into your daily life.

If you like this one, you may eventually want to try doing it with more complex tasks. When I'm in good meditating shape, I sometimes try (and often fail) to keep an accurate breath count while I drive to town, do an easy errand, and drive home. But start out with short, simple tasks, and if you lose count, you know what to do: Go directly to breath number one, without spending time on self-judgment or other thoughts!

The Walking Breath Meditation

Walk a bit more slowly than usual, focusing your attention on the ins and outs of your breath. Begin each inhale and each exhale with a mental label of "In" or "Out." Maintain a thumb to forefinger hand position, unless that feels unnatural now.

Without trying to control the breath too much, see if you can begin each in and each out breath exactly as one of your feet hits the ground. Notice how many steps you take during each inhalation, and how many steps you take during each exhalation.

Then count each step as you walk and breathe, so that in your mind you are saying "In two, three, four...Out two, three, four...In two, three, four...Out two, three, four" or perhaps "In two, three...Out two, three." Continue to substitute "In" or "Out" in place of each count of "one", to help you stay focused on the breathing as well as the walking.

Your own personal breathing rhythm may be different from the above. Your exhales may take longer than your inhales as in: "In two, three...Out two, three, four." Or your inhales may take longer than your exhales as in: "In two, three, four, five...Out two, three." The step count may vary from one breath to the next—just pay close attention, so that you can accurately count your steps during every inhale and every exhale. Just breathe, and walk, and count. As in all meditations, if your mind wanders, gently bring it back as soon as you notice that it's gone.

Using the Walking Breath Meditation in Real Life

I always use this meditation at the national publishing and music conventions, which tend to be hectic and stressful for me. Instead of scurrying and worrying from one appointment to the next, I walk and breathe, walk and breathe—so that each step soothes and centers my mind. Then, when I arrive at my next meeting, I'm more relaxed, and ready to deal with whatever may arise. Try it yourself, whether on a quiet walk in the country or in between errands on the job!

More Complex Clearing the Mind Meditations

In these following exercises, you'll be focusing your attention on a physical sensation, rather than merely labeling a physical action with a number as we've already done. Since this is a slightly less cut-and-dried thing to focus on, your attention is apt to wander more. So you must be diligent in noticing that the "puppy" of your attention is wandering off, and gently bring it back to the sound, or the foot, or the flame.

These meditations are somewhat harder to do during that boring meeting, or at the convention, since they require a bit more action than the simpler mind clearers. But with ingenuity, you'll find moments of privacy to practice the chant and slow walk, and candlelit restaurants are natural places to do a flame meditation (while your new date is in the rest room!)

About the Simple Chanting, or "Mantra," Meditation

This simple chanting, or "mantra" (a repeated sound used as a chant), exercise is probably the world's most widely used meditation. It's somewhat similar in nature to Maharishi Mahesh Yogi's Transcendental Meditation™, or "TM" system that The Beatles helped bring to the Western world in the late 1960s (except that it won't cost you $385, or require you to bring a white flower to the TM trainer). Dr. Herbert Benson further popularized this style of meditation in his "scientific" meditation book, cited earlier, *The Relaxation Response*. As I've mentioned, TM was my first organized meditation experience, and even though I no longer practice it, I'll always feel a debt of gratitude to both the Beatles and the Maharishi, for popularizing and publicizing this age-old technique in the West.

The Simple Chanting Meditation

Sit in a comfortable, upright position, in a quiet place. Place thumbs and forefingers together. Now focus your attention on a pleasant-sounding one- or-two syllable word. Yogis seem to prefer OM or AUM. Dr. Benson likes ONE. AMEN may be especially appropriate for those of a Christian persuasion. The TM folk also like two-syllable mantras (many of theirs sound quite like AMEN). Choose any one of these to use right now.

Begin by slowly whispering the word (let's say you've chosen OM) to yourself. Stop whispering "OM," and just think "OM." Perhaps you'll picture the word OM, written out in your mind. Perhaps you'll imagine hearing it in your mind, or imagine saying it. Keep your attention focused on that OM, in whatever form it may seem to appear.

Of course, your mind will wander. You'll find yourself thinking about tomorrow, or about how well-focused you are on the OM. Maybe you'll have a doubtful thought ("I can't do this") or a pleasant daydream.

When Attention Strays

When your attention strays from the OM, bring it gently but firmly back. Let go of the daydream, or the doubtful thought, or the desire thought for now. You can think about those things all you like, later. Now, you're just thinking OMMMM . . .

That's all there is to it. The more you do it, the longer you'll be able to stay with the OM. A few seconds at first, then ten, or fifteen, or half a minute. For many meditators, mantras seem to be an especially powerful focus for the attention. That's why they're so popular!

Christian, Jewish, and Buddhist Chants

If you enjoy practicing the Simple Chanting Meditation, you might eventually like to try repeating a longer chant. Some people find that a longer chant holds their attention more. Any short Christian prayer that you've memorized will work, like the "Prayer of the Heart": "Lord Jesus Christ, have mercy on me." If you come from the Hebraic tradition, try the most important prayer of the Jewish faith, the "Shma": "Hear oh Israel, the Lord our God, the Lord is One." (Pronounced: Shma' Yis-roy-el' Ah-doh-noy' Eh-lo-hay'-nu, Ah-doh-noy' Eh-chord').

The Buddha's last instructions to his disciples were to repeatedly chant the phrase "Nam Myoho Renge Kyo" (Pronounced: Nahm Me-yo'-ho Reng'-yay Ke-yo'). A greatly oversimplified translation of this might be, "I devote myself to the law of the Universal Consciousness." This form of meditation is now known as "Nichiren" Buddhism, and has proponents and groups world-wide.

Consult your local priest or rabbi to obtain additional Judaic or Christian chants, which will add greater depth to the practice of your chosen religion. You might also look up Jim Cowan's book on Nichiren Buddhism in the bibliography, or create a meaningful chant of your own.

The Slow Walking Meditation

You'll probably want to begin practicing this one in a private place, since it looks a bit funny. Pick a spot where you can walk for at least eight or ten feet in a straight line.

Now walk *very* slowly, so slowly that you have enough time to mentally label *every part* of every step.

Say "lifting" as you pick your foot up. Say "moving" as your foot travels through the air. Say "placing" as you put that foot down again. Say "shifting" as you shift your weight onto that foot. Say "lifting" as you begin to pick up the other foot. And so on. Lifting, moving, placing, shifting . . . lifting, moving, placing, shifting . . .

At first, take a minimum of eight to ten seconds to complete each four-part (lifting, moving, placing, shifting) step. This is truly life in the slow lane! Whenever your attention wanders, bring it back to your walking process.

As you get used to focusing on your feet, you can try some-times walking faster, labeling only the lifting and placing portions of each step. If you prefer, you can say "up" and "down" instead of "lift" and "place." Or try slowing it way down, and take thirty to forty seconds (some people call this "the Zombie Walk") for every complete step.

Other thoughts intruding? Get right back to that focus on the active foot!

The Flame Meditation

In a darkened room, from ten or fifteen inches away, stare intently at a candle's flame for one or two minutes. Whenever your attention wanders, return your gaze to the heart of that tiny fire. Try not to think about the candle, or this exercise, or why fire looks as it does, or politics. Just keep returning your attention to stare at the flame.

Abruptly blow the candle out, and close your eyes. Within a few seconds, you'll begin to see the image of the flame again, apparently projected onto the inside of your eyelids. Watch that image for as long as you can. It may change color, or shape, or seem to slide around. It may disappear, and then come back in a slightly different shape, color, or form. But you'll recognize it, if you concentrate. With practice, you'll be able to perceive the image for at least as long as you watched the actual flame.

I find the combination of focusing on both the real flame and then the afterimage exciting and challenging. Artists and other people who are visually oriented may achieve an exceptionally strong concentration with this exercise.

For Friends and Couples: The "Ahhh" Breath

For a very intimate experience with a close friend, relative, or lover, try this exercise. I learned it from Stephen Levine, who learned it from Richard Boerstler, of The Clear Light Society. I don't know who Richard learned it from, but it's a wonderful thing to do!

Decide which of you will be the active partner. The inactive partner simply sits or lies comfortably, eyes closed, and breathes normally. The active partner sits nearby, close enough to see the rising and falling of the inactive partner's chest as they breathe, close enough to hear each in and out breath.

The active partner tries to match as exactly as possible the breathing rhythm of the other, to begin the in breath exactly as they do, to inhale exactly as long, to hold the breath exactly as long, to exhale for the same amount of time. It's not easy to do, and requires intense concentration! On each exhale, the active partner will release the breath with a sigh . . . "ahhh."

The inactive partner should try not to "help" the active partner by making breaths unusually regular or loud, neither should they try to hinder the other by holding their breath or breathing especially softly.

This exercise promotes a strong feeling of connection, compassion, and love between the partners. It's almost as though one breath is being shared between two people—sometimes it actually feels as though the two bodies are somehow merged. Couples will find this a lovely trust-builder, and especially powerful if eye contact is maintained. You can even do the "ahhh" breath with a pet (you'll probably need to take the active role).

Many nurses, therapists, and some physicians use this meditation with their patients. It can be done with the inactive partner sleeping or comatose, and may be very calming and soothing for someone who is ill, as well as for the healer.

The Heartbeat Meditation

Every second your heart beats at least once. If it stops beating for very long, you're history. So counting or labeling each beat is an amazingly powerful attention focuser, even if you only do it for one minute or less. If you are a hypochondriac, or have any heart problems, don't do this exercise until you feel very comfortable with the mind-watching exercises that follow.

Put your hand over your heart, or locate the pulse in your wrist with a few fingers. Count each beat or pulse to four, or ten, like you've done with the breath. If you lose count, start again.

Or label each beat or pulse by mentally saying "beat" every time you feel one. This is similar to what you did with the four-part walking meditation.

For me, the exciting (and scary) part of this meditation is that my heart skips a beat every minute or two. I'm never absolutely certain whether the next beat will happen, or not. So I have to pay very close attention.

Doctors tell me that unless you average more than four or five per minute, skipped beats are not necessarily indicative of heart problems. But it's still a bit unnerving, when it occurs. If a fear thought comes up after a skipped beat, just notice it, notice that you've stopped counting or labeling, then go back to focus on the heartbeat. You can always worry later, after you're done meditating. Or, perhaps, with sufficient meditation, you won't even want to worry quite as much!

Harder Walking and Breathing Meditations

These next two mind clearers involve the focus of attention directly on physical sensations, no counting or labeling. They are the mainstays of the Vipassana meditative tradition. If they seem hard to concentrate on, alternate them with exercises that you find easier, like the meditations above.

The No-Label Walking Meditation

Walk slowly, and focus your attention carefully on your feet. What does walking really feel like? Which muscles in your calves, ankles, or toes do you use? What is the consistency of the ground—is it hard, or rough, or spongy? Go barefoot, and feel each pebble, twig, or crack in the floor.

You may find it easier to begin with this meditation by doing the Walking Breath or the Slow Walk (labeling) Meditation. After a minute of those, stop counting breaths or labeling, and focus on your feet and the ground. As usual, when thoughts intrude, gently return your attention to your feet.

The No-Label Breath Meditation

Breathe normally, and focus your attention on the sensation of breathing. In what part of your body do you feel each inhale most clearly? Some people feel the breath best at the nostrils, right where it flows in and out. Others find it easier to concentrate on the rise and fall of the stomach or chest. Mouth breathers might be very aware of the breath at the back of the throat. Choose one of these areas, and concentrate on it.

Do not try to control your breathing at all, to make it slow, or even, or otherwise meditative. Just let every breath be exactly as it is.

Observe *each* breath as though it were a strange and unique creature passing in front of you. Is this breath long, or short? Smooth and continuous, or jerky? Feel cool, or hot? Does it go directly from inhale to exhale, or is there a point at which the breath is held immobile? Was there a cough, burp, or hiccup experienced as part of this breath? Or even a sneeze (my favorite special breath effect, see page 39). A sighing or wheezing quality to it? As always, if your attention wanders off, return it diligently but gently to the breath.

Helpful Hint: Wavy Gravy (clown, prankster, and sixties holdout) works with dying children in San Francisco. His meditation practice helps him to stay calm and loving, in the hospital or in the circus. He likes to put a touch of "Tiger Balm" liniment (or Vicks Vaporub) inside the big red ball of his clown nose as an aid to concentrating on the sensation of the breath at the nostrils. Try it!

The Tongue-Block Breath Meditation

This easy but effective meditation comes out of both the harmonica and the yogic traditions. When playing harmonica, "tongue blocking" is a method of playing low and high notes simultaneously by blocking out the middle notes with the tip of the tongue. In my "Zen and the Art of Blues Harmonica" workshops, I've noticed that many students find tongue blocking to be an excellent attention focuser. In the popular Kriya yoga style, an important technique involves placing the tongue tip so that it partially blocks the incoming air, which helps emphasize attention on the breath.

Just touch the tip of your tongue to the roof of your mouth, less than an inch behind your upper front teeth. As you inhale, you'll feel the coolness of each breath on the sensitive underside of your tongue. You can apply this new tongue position to any of the breathing meditations: the basic, the chore-based, or the no-label (for which it may be especially useful). And it's inconspicuous enough to do anywhere or anytime (which, of course, is where you *should* be doing it!).

Looking and Listening Meditations

Our last (and perhaps most difficult) type of mind-clearing exercise is to watch clouds, or the flames of a fire, or the foaming waves at the ocean's shore. Don't try to make sense of what you see. Don't try to look for patterns. Don't judge what you're seeing. Do nothing but see. Just seeing. As soon as you notice a thought creeping into your mind, go back to just seeing.

It's easiest to begin Looking Meditations with natural objects like those mentioned above, as they are slightly less likely to inspire thoughts in your mind than visual objects like faces or bodies are. But with practice, you will be able to look at anything and "just see." Cars or people passing by, a blank wall, or your own hands can provide visual objects for the focus of your attention.

You can practice *listening* in the same way. No thought, no judging, no attempts to make sense. Just listening. If thoughts intrude, notice that you're thinking, then focus your attention back to the music. Instrumental music is usually the easiest type of meditative listening to begin with, as any music that contains words tends to inspire thought when you hear the lyrics.

Of course, when you've *really* gotten the hang of it, *everywhere* that you go and *everything* that you do can become the basis for a mind-clearing meditation. We can call this rather advanced state "Living in the Now," and it will be examined in greater detail later on in this book.

Watching the Mind

I've written so much about watching the mind in Part One of this book that I don't have much to say about it here. If you've begun doing the mind-*clearing* exercises, then you're probably ready to try some mind *watching*. It might be useful to read my earlier section on mind watching, pages 35 to 38, before doing the following exercises. I'd also highly recommend Stephen Levine's book *A Gradual Awakening*, which has a great deal to say about the subtle art of mind watching.

In these exercises, *thoughts in the mind* will provide the focal point for our attention. In other words, we'll be using thoughts as our meditation objects, just as we've already used breathing and walking. As with the breathing and walking exercises, we'll begin by counting, and then by labeling, our thoughts. Finally, we'll be able to focus on the direct sensations that our thoughts produce, without counting or labeling.

The Thought-Counting Meditation

This exercise will help you to start withdrawing your attention from the *content* of your thoughts, as discussed on page 36.

Sit comfortably, with some type of timer or alarm clock handy. If none are available, make sure you can see a clock. Set the timer for one minute, or time yourself by the clock.

Now close your eyes, and begin to count your thoughts. As soon as a thought appears in your mind, count it, but don't "get into" the content of that thought. If you do, you may only end up with a count of one thought for your entire minute!

Think about a bird-watching competition. Competitive bird watchers go out, armed with binoculars, to try to identify as many species of bird as they can in one day. They don't study each bird for hours, or even minutes. As soon as they see one—that's it—on to look for the next. And you're a thought watcher, for these sixty seconds!

You've already gained some skill at returning the focus of your attention to a meditation (from practicing the mind clearing meditations). So you'll probably be able to let go of each thought after counting it, unless it's one of those particularly stubborn thoughts, which we'll deal with below. And then return the focus of your attention towards looking for another thought to count. If no thoughts seem to come up, either say to yourself "no thoughts" (which is a perfectly valid thought itself, and should be counted), or else just relax and enjoy a moment of spontaneous mind clearing!

So keep a count of your thoughts. This will include thoughts such as "gee, I haven't had many thoughts yet" or "uh-oh, was that thought number seven or number eight?" Some thoughts will flash by like speedy and exotic birds, perhaps as quick mental pictures or even as single words. Others will lumber like penguins into sight of your mind's eye, and take their time leaving as well.

If a thought arises, and its content is so "grabby" for you that you just "can't" let go of it, try to remember what thought it is. That information will be useful, even though it seems to be preventing you from doing this exercise right now. Write the stubborn thought down, then try the exercise again later on. Fear thoughts and desire thoughts tend to be the hardest to let go of, for most people. But remember—it's not the fear or the desire thought that's the problem—it is the inability to control your reaction to that thought that may create a problem.

This isn't an easy exercise, but there is no way to do it wrong. It's sole purpose is to learn to look, for this moment, at your thoughts as objects, like birds, or rocks, or other people. Nothing to take personally—just thoughts.

About the Thought-Labeling Meditation

In the last meditation, we paid *no* attention to the content of the thoughts that we were counting. Now, we are going to pay just barely enough attention to thought content so that we will be able to *label* each thought.

Now make a brief mental or written list of the *types* or categories of thoughts that are commonly featured in the movie of your mind. I have about eight perennial favorites, which I'll list below, in general order of popularity. Is your list as high-minded and spiritual as mine?

Planning thoughts are those in which I try to decide exactly what to do, specifically ("I'll write to John, then have lunch") or generally ("perhaps I should go to law school"). Desire thoughts include wishes for anything, from sex to world peace. Fear thoughts include any type of worry: hypochondria, money, work, you name it. Happy or appreciative thoughts are often noting pleasurable sensations such as the sun on my face, or the smell of potatoes cooking. Judging thoughts are those in which I approve or, more likely, criticize anything or anyone. Righteous thoughts are those in which I am right, and someone else is wrong. Angry thoughts could be those directed at myself, in which case I consider them as falling into the specialized subcategory of self-hating thoughts, or at anybody else.

The Thought-Labeling Meditation

Sit comfortably, and observe each thought as it swims into awareness. Observe it only long enough to decide which one of your categories it fits into, then go on to look for the next. If absolutely no thoughts seem to be forthcoming right now, simply relax and enjoy a few seconds of effortless mind clearing.

If a thought doesn't seem to fit into any of your categories, just make up a more or less appropriate new category, ("ahh, that's one of those 'What-If-I-Had-Been-Born-an-Eskimo' type of thoughts") and go back to looking for the next thought.

As in the last exercise, if a "grabby" thought arises, just notice what thought, and type of thought, it is.

After the meditation, see if you can tell which thoughts occurred most often. Which thoughts were easy to let go of? Which ones were hard to let go of?

The Particular Thought-Counting Meditation

You can choose any thought, or category of thought, to notice in this exercise. You will probably get the most benefits by choosing one of those "grabby" thoughts, as they are the thoughts that you most need practice working with.

In this exercise, you are going to try to remember to count the number of times in the course of an hour or a day that a particular thought arises. That's all there is to it. You may want to keep count on a piece of paper, so that you don't forget your score. Try not to get angry with yourself for having these uncontrollable thoughts. The Compassion exercises later on will help you to treat even your own mind with a touch of mercy . . .

I usually do this exercise with my righteous thoughts, since they are, for me, the grabbiest. I love to be *right*, and it's hard for me to let someone else be wrong without their admitting it, to just let go of me being right and them being wrong. On a seriously righteous day, I can count dozens of righteous thoughts! Doing so helps me to be aware of the hold that this particular thought has on me, and to diminish it.

The "Rube Goldberg" Thought Chain Meditation

In a Rube Goldberg cartoon, strange events are chained together to cause a final event. To create a Goldberg alarm clock, for example, the sun comes up, and its rays through a magnifying glass burn the rope that holds up the cheese, the cheese falls down so that the mice come out, the cat goes after the mice, the dog goes after the cat from under the bed where he was sleeping, which pulls out a slat so that the farmer falls on the floor and is woken up in time for milking!

Our minds often work similarly, chaining together thoughts in strange ways. As I began to observe my thoughts more carefully, I found that my frustration or fear thoughts usually bring up anger thoughts, as I described in the "Rambo Mind" (page 39) and "Applying Compassion to Thoughts" (page 45) sections.

After you've spent some time with the Thought-Counting and Thought-Labeling Meditations, try a Thought-Labeling exercise in which you specifically look for two or more thoughts which often occur together. You may find for example, that the guilt thoughts that you had perceived as happening spontaneously are actually a result of prior angry thoughts, which themselves are a result of helplessness thoughts. Becoming aware of your thoughts in this manner can really help you to understand why you feel the way you do.

The Experiencing Thoughts Meditation

Just as with breathing and walking, we began by counting our thoughts, and then labeling them. Now it's time to just experience the sensation of thoughts, rather as we experienced the physical sensations of walking and breathing in the "no-label" walking and breathing exercises.

Begin with a moment of your favorite meditation, just to relax and clear your mind a bit. Then call one of your "grabby" thoughts, perhaps a fear, or a desire, or an anger into your mind. Observe the thought, and ask yourself, "What does anger (or whatever) feel like?" Is it a hot feeling, or a cool feeling? Does my body feel tighter, or looser? Is there an enjoyable element to this feeling, or is it only painful?

Just watch the thought—step back, and turn it around in your mind like an object that you are investigating. It might be useful to reread my sections "At the Movies" and "Relating to Your Mind" from Part One now (page 37). Does looking at the thought in this way change your reaction to the thought? In what way?

If you find yourself getting caught up in the content of the thought ("I have a right to be angry, they shouldn't have . . ."), watch the caught-up-ness. How does it feel to be caught up in a thought like that? And if you cannot back off and relate *to* this particular thought, try one that's not so grabby for now!

Living in the Now

Most of us live most of the time in either the past or the future. Only rarely is our attention focused on what is happening in the "Right Now." Is yours? You think so? Then quick—without thinking about it—are you inhaling or exhaling? You probably had to refocus your attention onto the breath to answer that question. Where had it been?

Thoughts about what we just did, or didn't do, and thoughts about what we should do, or shouldn't do, or might do, continually clutter our minds. How often we use past thoughts in a self-hating way, "I should have done it differently," or "I sure messed that one up." How often we use future thoughts to upset ourselves, such as "What if that happens?" or "It probably won't work out."

Virtually all of our thoughts are either based in past or future, and absolutely all of our fears and desires. Desires are usually remembrances of past pleasures that we plan and hope to recreate in the future. Fears are usually memories of past pain that we plan and hope to avoid in the future.

In a way, all of the exercises are "Living in the Now" exercises. When we are Thought Counting or Slow Walking, there just isn't much time to think of the past or the future. We learn to let go of such thoughts, as soon as we notice them.

There is something very satisfying about keeping your mind in the Now, but it's hard to describe it precisely. All I can say is that the bite of food that you are savoring right *now*, is somehow quite different from the mouthful that you just ate (which you can only remember) or the mouthful that you plan to eat next (which you can only anticipate). Of course, thinking about either the past or future mouthful does bring it into the Now as a *thought* in your mind. But the actual food that's in your mouth can clearly be more satisfying than the thought of past or future food which may be in your mind right now. Better to be present with a potato than lost in thoughts of past or future banquets!

As a small press publisher, I often need to plan books, advertising, or marketing strategies far into the future. So my Now may involve initiating events that will not be completed for many months. It's confusing for me to separate the reality of the "publisher's Now" (which includes the next six to twelve months) from my "personal Now." In my personal Now I wish to savor the events of the present—smells, tastes, feelings—without overinfluence by future and past related fears and desires. It's a delicate balance, and one that I don't yet clearly understand. But I do know that the following "Living in the Now" exercises help! And, speaking of a delicate balance . . .

The Centering Balance Meditation

Stand up straight, arms at your sides, with your feet no more than six inches apart. Focus your attention on your sense of balance, your sensation of standing upright with your body weight centered over your feet.

Lean forward an inch or two, and feel the tension as your toes dig deeper into the ground to compensate for the forward incline, as you become a human Tower of Pisa. Lean backwards an inch, until most of your weight is on your heels. Lean slightly left and then right, noting the weight shift from foot to foot.

Do the forwards, backwards, left, and right leaning motions again, but more subtly, with less movement. See just how little you need to lean in order to feel not quite perfectly upright, not quite perfectly balanced. See how easy it is to overcompensate, in one direction or another. Is there any one position in which you do feel in *complete* equilibrium, when you really focus your attention on it? There may not be one.

You can do this exercise anywhere, without attracting much attention to yourself, if you use the more subtle motions of the second part. Since "feeling balanced" is often used as a metaphor for mental stability, this exercise is a useful one to do anytime you feel off-balance. The few moments' respite that you'll get from the tensions of past and future thoughts will help you to restore both your mental and physical equilibrium!

Other Living-in-the-Now Meditations

We can also take commonplace daily activities and easily convert them into effective and interesting Living-in-the-Now Meditations. In effect, we've already done this with walking and breathing. As I've said before, *anything* done with a high degree of focused awareness is, by definition, a meditation.

The Zen Buddhist tradition of Japan often utilized this approach. Flower arranging, the Tea Ceremony, Zen archery, and most of the Japanese martial arts are used as forms of meditation. Their practitioners focus exclusively on the flowers, or tea, or bow, excluding all other thoughts. Sound familiar?

The Conscious Eating Meditation

Our society gives us many mixed messages about food. We use it to give ourselves love by eating exotic chocolates, tantalizing treats, and tempting tidbits. Yet we also punish ourselves and use food to withhold self-approval, with crash diets and lifelong obsessions about those few extra pounds of flab. We pay lots of attention to what we eat, but little to how we feel while we eat. Often we avoid feeling entirely while eating. We do this by eating and conversing in the company of others, and when alone will eat while reading, or in front of the television set. Or we may stuff ourselves compulsively without even tasting the food.

A conscious focus of attention on feeling and eating can be a most powerful experience. Someday, perhaps when eating by yourself, try this Conscious Eating Meditation.

Once your food is in front of you, spend a moment with a mind-clearing exercise, perhaps one of the breath-based meditations. Then, slowly, begin to eat. Focus your attention on each part of the eating process, lifting the fork or spoon, choosing which forkful of food to pick up, lifting the food to your mouth, placing the food in your mouth, lowering the fork, chewing the food and noticing the taste, swallowing the food, then lifting the fork once again.

If you like, label each action, as you did in the Slow Walking Meditation: lifting, choosing, lifting, placing, lowering, chewing, tasting, and swallowing. If other labels seem more appropriate to you, by all means use your own.

Perhaps you would prefer to concentrate on how each action feels, rather than labeling them, as you did in the No-Label Walking Meditation. Simply slow down and concentrate on your eating. Some people find that this is easier to do if they hold their fork in the hand that they don't usually use, as this will increase your concentration on your fork hand.

Notice the sensation of metal against mouth, the muscular actions involved in lifting, chewing, swallowing. Feel each motion of your tongue, your lips, your throat. Concentrate on the texture and taste of each food. Be as specific as possible in your investigation. Do the skins of peas taste different from the insides? How close to your mouth is the food before you smell it? What else can you notice?

As usual, be aware of thoughts as they arise in the mind, and then return your attention to your food. I often notice a desire to choose and lift the next forkful before I'm done chewing and swallowing the one in my mouth. This desire is then usually followed by a guilty thought about greediness. If similar thoughts occur to you, note them, perhaps label them ("aha, there's greed . . ."), then let them pass, and return mindfully to your dinner. If sad or lonely thoughts (especially around eating alone) come to you, as they often do to me in the course of this meditation, a moment of one of the Compassion Exercises (page 104) may well be in order.

An interesting duo exercise for friends or couples is to take turns feeding each other, while silently focusing on physical or mental sensations. For me, this usually stirs up compassionate feelings as the feeder, and vulnerable or infantile feelings as the one being fed.

Conscious Driving

Driving is one of the most hazardous things we do on a daily basis. Yet often, as we drive, our mind is lost in the past or the future, far from a clear focus on the manipulation of tons of iron at high rates of speed. We talk, listen to the radio, eat, drink or smoke, keeping "half an eye" on the road and other traffic.

In conscious driving, we focus our attention exclusively on the elements important to automotive safety, as intently as though we were Monte Carlo racing drivers, participating in the race of our lives. But instead of concentrating on speed alone, we pay attention to many factors: the road in front of us, the positions of other cars near us, our speed, driving conditions, and road conditions.

Should any thoughts *not* germane only to safe driving enter, we notice them and gently return our attention to our driving. If this exercise seems, for any reason, to be unsafe, please don't do it. But I am convinced that if more people did focus their attention exclusively on their driving, that the highways would be much safer places.

More Living-in-the-Now Meditations

As I've said throughout this book, we can make any activity a meditation simply by steadily focusing our attention on it. Try doing this with shaving, brushing your teeth (I find that switching hands here really forces me to focus on my hand movements, and makes the toothbrush meditation a challenge), washing your hands, dishes, or any other simple daily task.

Just make sure that you are thinking only of the task at hand, and gently return your awareness to it as soon as you notice other thoughts entering the mind.

I like to try to make hand washing into a meditation, each time I do it throughout the day. Instead of using those thirty or forty seconds to plan, or worry, or daydream, I focus on the sensations of warmth, wetness, slipperiness, rinsing, drying. And feel better centered and more relaxed afterwards. Perhaps cleanliness is next to godliness, after all!

Visualization

The fact that our brains and bodies react so strongly to pictures in the mind's eye makes the ability to visualize very important. A tremendous amount of evidence indicates that after we've spent some time clearly visualizing ourselves performing an activity, it actually becomes easier for us to do. This technique works in almost any sphere, from athletics to music to relaxation, and the key element seems to be the degree of "real-ness" of the visualization. So it clearly pays to spend some time practicing and strengthening this most useful skill.

In a way, the term *visual*ization is a bit of a misnomer, since this technique's effectiveness is increased when senses other than the visual can be incorporated into every exercise. In the following exercise, try to recreate, in your mind, a vivid sense of sight, feel, smell, and taste.

If the idea of learning more about visualization appeals to you, I'd suggest three books to begin with: *Super-Learning, Psycho-Cybernetics,* and *The Silva Mind Control Method* (see bibliography).

The Lemon Meditation

Picture a lemon in your mind's eye, as clearly as possible. As yellow as the sun, its thick skin minutely wrinkled, and just a touch oily to the hand. Dig your fingernail into the peel, and see a tiny spray of citric oil arch out into the air. Pull some peel off, to expose the white fibers covering the juicy, wet, pulpy, insides.

You smell the tartness as you bite deep into the lemon, and taste the sourness. The saliva leaps into your mouth.

If you were able to visualize the lemon with any clarity, you probably salivated even before you imagined biting into it. And that's the point of this "Body/Mind" exercise.

Most people would consider salivation to be a bodily process outside of their conscious control. And yet we salivate when we think of lemons. Just the thought of the taste of citrus somehow stimulates a gland in the mouth to produce a secretion.

Practice your visualization with this lemon exercise. Can you "train" your salivary glands to spring into action at the first thought of lemon? At the word "lemon"? We'll continue to use visualization skills in many of the exercises, so practice a few more.

How about some *wild* visualizations, just for fun? Can you picture Frankenstein's monster? Now put him into a tuxedo! Change the tux to a yellow tutu! Make him do the Charleston, then replace him with an image of . . . Robert Redford! When will we ever stop having fun?!!!

The Meditation Visualization Exercise

This exercise is a warm-up for the Master Skill exercise at the end of the book. Spend just twenty or thirty seconds (or more) a few times each day, picturing yourself *actually using* a Three Minute Meditation technique in a real-life situation. For instance, you might picture yourself doing one of the walking meditations as you return to the office from lunch. Try to experience the scene that you've mentally created as clearly as possible. Feel your feet as they hit the floor, and feel your thumbs gently touching your fore-fingers. See the surrounding area, and hear or smell any appropriate sounds or odors.

After you've done this a few times, try to visualize using meditation to deal with a slightly more stressful scenario. Perhaps you can *picture* using a walking meditation on the way to the boss's office for a meeting, or on the way to a blind date!

Once you feel comfortable with the above exercises, jump to the back of the book, and try the Master Skill Meditation!

Visualization and Health

For thousands of years, the fakirs of India have demonstrated their abilities to control various bodily functions to an astounding degree. Using techniques of a meditative type, a top-shelf fakir can suspend respiratory and circulatory functions for prolonged periods of time, and even a run-of-the-mill one can lie on a bed of nails or walk on burning coals. So it appears that the mind has a far greater degree of control over the body than is generally believed in the West.

A number of new body/mind sciences, such as Psycho-Neuro-Immunology (PNI) deal with just this subject. If people can mentally control a glandular secretion like saliva (just as you did in the Lemon exercise), why *shouldn't* we be able to stimulate or retard other glandular functions, or rebuild a damaged immune system? The preliminary evidence indicates that we can, and visualization is the technique most often used! If this subject interests you, I recommend reading Joan Borysenko's *Minding the Body, Mending the Mind*, and Bernie Siegal's *Love, Medicine, and Miracles* (see bibliography).

Of course, the body/mind connection does not *only* manifest itself in exotic or miraculous ways. Every time you raise a finger, or take a step, a thought in your mind is somehow motivating a physical response in your body. The ordinary things that we do every day never seem quite as wonderful as someone else's feats. But, is the ability to *not* breathe on demand any more impressive than its opposite? Just because everybody can do it, makes it no less magical!

Relaxation

Being able to relax the muscles of the body at will is a useful ability, and one that visualization skills can help with. You may find it easiest, in the beginning, to practice this exercise while lying in bed, face up, and arms at your sides. Take as long as you need, the first few times you do it, perhaps ten or twenty minutes.

Make fists with both hands. Really clench your fingers into your palms. Feel the tightness in your wrists, and even up into your forearms. Hold the tension for five or six seconds, then relax it. Tense up again, for a similar amount of time, then relax. This time, as you relax your hands, say "warm and heavy, warm and heavy" to yourself, and visualize your hands feeling warm and heavy, just sinking heavily into the softness of the bed. I like to picture my hands being made of mercury, or molten lead, warm and soft and very heavy.

Perform this same process—tensing and relaxing, then tensing and relaxing, and saying "warm and heavy" (with appropriate warm and heavy visualizations)—for each major muscle group of your body. After doing your hands, do your feet, calves, thighs, buttocks, stomach, chest, arms, shoulders, neck, jaw, and eyes. Tense and relax, tense and relax. Warm and heavy, warm and heavy. Try to cultivate as relaxed a feeling as you can, throughout your entire body.

Once you feel really relaxed, imagine yourself in a very peaceful place, a place that you associate with relaxation. Try to develop as clear a mental picture as possible of this place, including the way it feels, sounds, looks, smells, and even tastes. Memorize as many details as you can. I visualize a lovely, tropical beach. I feel the warm sun and the cool breeze, and the sand under me, as I look up at the waving palm fronds. I hear the waves crash, and smell, almost taste, the salt spray in the air.

After you've done this exercise a few times, you'll find yourself able to mentally recreate your relaxation place, and feel relaxed, without needing to do the tensing and relaxing, or at least not needing to do it for so long. With practice, you'll be able to return to your relaxing spot just by thinking of it for a second or two. Whenever you're under stress, you'll be able to take an instant vacation, without even moving!

Compassion

As I've said before, compassion is the heart of meditation. Because without it, meditation is all too likely to become just another activity that we do "wrong," or "don't do enough" of, or "should be attaining quicker results" from.

It's important to differentiate compassion from pity, which I try to do by this criteria: In pity, there is an element of fear for oneself. We see the accident victim and our feelings of empathy are tinged with fear for ourselves ("Gee, that could have happened to me—I'm glad it didn't, and sure hope that it doesn't"). In compassion, there is a wry acceptance of the human condition that we all share, and no attempt to distance the negative events by making them "something that happens to someone else."

These above are rather fine points, and perhaps will help you to sort out pity/compassion feelings that you experience. The following are the compassion meditations that I find most useful and satisfying.

The Heartgill Meditation

I believe that I came up with this meditation myself, or at least its central image, one night while I was meditating next to my tropical-fish tank. I focused my attention on my pet angelfish, "Miss Piggy," and observed her bulging eyes and softly billowing gills. Then I imagined that my heart was somehow like a "compassion gill," and with each breath in and out, a wave of compassion washed through me, cleaning out pain and self-hating thoughts, and replacing them with compassion.

Although from an analytical perspective it may seem silly, it feels quite satisfying, somehow. Just "relocate" the in and out of your breath from the nostrils to the heart. Visualize a gill slit, like a fish's, right above the heart in your chest, and let the compassion wash through you, like the water washes through the fish with its life-giving oxygen. As with every other meditation that we've done, when other thoughts arise, simply notice them, and gently return to the image of the heartgill.

And please realize that it's easy to create meditations of your own. They don't have to be traditional in any way, or even make sense. They just have to feel right to you.

The Ahhh/Oooh Meditation

This one integrates both awe and pain, by seeing each as necessary to the other. In a world of beauty and splendor, how can there not be awe? But in a world where everyone who is born must die, how can there not be pain? And in a world filled with both pain and awe, how can there not be compassion for those who must live there?

As you breathe in, say a mental "Ahhh," the "Ahhh" of going outside on a beautiful spring morning, the "Ahhh" of watching the sun set over the ocean.

As you breathe out, groan "Oooh," the "Oooh" of seeing a war on television, the "Oooh" of seeing homeless people rummage for food in garbage dumpsters. "Ahhh, Oooh, Ahhh, Oooh." It's painful, living in this strange, lovely, terrible, unfathomable world. It's awesome, living in this strange, lovely, terrible, unfathomable world. The two just can't be separated. How can you not feel compassion for any creature who must exist here, including yourself?

The Forgiveness Meditation

This one is very simple, although not always easy. Just picture someone whom you think has hurt or wronged you in some way. It's important, for now, to choose someone at whom you're no longer very angry. Visualize them as clearly as you can. And tell them "I forgive you. I forgive you for hurting or wronging me."

Repeat it a number of times, and try to feel forgiving, try to feel yourself giving up remnants of anger or righteousness towards them. If you are not sure with whom you're ready to do this exercise, do it with someone whose hurt to you was very minor—a driver who slipped ahead of you on the freeway, or a clerk who overcharged you by a few cents. Eventually, with practice, you'll be able to do this exercise with people who have caused you more serious pain.

It's crucial to remember that forgiving a person does *not* mean that you condone or accept their behavior. You are forgiving the person, not their behavior. And letting go of anger, and of feelings of having been wronged, is a very freeing experience. For me, doing this exercise on the publisher who had "appropriated" my harmonica book and title concept (see "Why I Needed to Meditate") allowed me to stop wasting energy on anger and self-hatred, and to get on with my life.

The next exercise is somewhat tied in to this one, and may make a sense of forgiveness easier to come by. You can also combine the two, to develop a deeper sense of understanding and compassion for the chosen subject of the meditation.

The I-Thou Meditation

Jewish theologian Martin Buber coined the term "I-Thou," to indicate a relationship in which you (the "I") relate to another person with the understanding that the other has as many feelings and needs, fears and desires, as you do, and as much right to pursue them. Buber contrasts this with the "I-It" relationship, in which you act as though the other person is mostly an object, whose principle purpose in life is to help you gain satisfaction.

It's easy to be smug, and to say "I don't do *that*." But how often, especially when you're in a hurry, does a store clerk or a gas-station attendant seem to be a real, complete person with their own history and feelings? When someone cuts ahead of you on line, do you usually perceive them as a person who has problems, fears, and needs of their own, just as you do, or are they just some "impolite jerk," getting in between you and the candy counter? Can you see that the beautiful woman, or "hunky" man walking across the street has a full and complete life of their own, and does not just exist as an object for your visual (or perhaps fantasized sexual) gratification?

Begin by choosing someone, a bank teller, or door-to-door salesperson, to whom you usually *don't* relate, and try to perceive them as a "thou" instead of an "it." With a bit of practice, you'll be able to do this with a surly waiter, an aggressive panhandler, or a politician not from the party of your choice! And doing so may just help you with the next exercise, which is of tremendous importance to you!

The Compassion Exercise

Picture yourself as a small child at the youngest age that you can remember. Visualize your child-self as clearly as possible, then send feelings of love and compassion to that small child-self. Wrap your arms around yourself, or at least place one hand over the other in a loving, compassionate way. In your mind's eye, see yourself hugging your child-self.

If feelings or thoughts other than love and compassion enter, gently return your mind to thoughts of love and compassion for your child-self.

For many of us, compassionate feelings for ourselves at any age do not come easily. Do this exercise with as much loving kindness as you can muster, and try not to be judgmental if it seems difficult. Can you see the irony of judging yourself harshly for not being able to do a compassion exercise "perfectly enough"? Just do the best that you can, and recognize that it will become easier with time.

I often find judgmental thoughts such as, "I don't deserve this," or "The kid's gotta be tough" creeping in during this exercise. I've gotten lots of practice at noticing them quickly, and learned to use them as a springboard to lend renewed vigor to my feelings of compassion. Instead of increasing pain, these self-hating thoughts can be used as a stepping stone towards increased self-love by saying, "I've been so hard on myself, for so long, that I can scarcely do this exercise at all. I need as much love and compassion as I can allow myself."

Next, picture yourself as an older child, and do the same thing. Don't forget to hug yourself, at least in your mind. Move up to puberty (an age where we all especially need compassion, and hugs) and do it, then in steps of five or ten years until you reach your present age. Now do the same thing you've been doing for younger selves—bathe yourself in love and compassion, while hugging yourself. Only this time, do it right now, with your own arms wrapped lovingly around yourself.

If you feel resistant to doing this exercise, examine your resistance. How does it feel? Could you do the "I-Thou" for others, but not be able to do this one for yourself? How does that fact touch you? Perhaps you need to first do the Forgiveness meditation for *yourself,* or for a parent who has taught you to be self-critical rather than compassionate. If you can't seem to do this Compassion exercise at all, see Theodore Isaac Rubin's book *Compassion and Self-Hate.*

The Zen of "Don't Know"

At the heart of traditional Japanese Zen Style meditation is the "koan." A koan is a question with no rational answer. Some favorite traditional koans are:

"What is the sound of one hand clapping?"

"What did your face look like before your mother's birth?"

"Can a dog achieve enlightenment?"

Observe your mind as you focus your attention on one of these questions. Does it strive for an answer? Does it want to reject the exercise by calling it ridiculous?

Try to cultivate a sense of "don't know." It may not feel comfortable, at first. But just let it be okay *not* to know. Look for the empty, spacious feeling of the "don't know" mind. The "don't know" mind has room for absolutely everything!

The standard story used to illustrate this concept tells of the scientist who visited the Buddhist teacher, in order to learn about Buddhism from a "scientific" point of view. Before beginning, the Buddhist suggested having tea. He filled the scientist's teacup to the brim, paused for a second, then poured more tea into the cup. The scientist leaped up as the hot tea cascaded into his lap. "A teacup that is too full," the Buddhist said, "can receive nothing additional. Neither can a mind."

Jesus' statement "Before Abraham was, I am" (John 8:58) makes a wonderful Christian koan! And since the word that Jesus used for "I am" was also the sacred name for God, it fits in well with some concepts that I'll later present in the "I Am" section of the book.

Since childhood, I've enjoyed pondering the koan, "Ice cream has no bones." And that, of course, is a classic ice-cream koan (apologies to Ben Cohen & Jerry Greenfield)!

The Don't Know Meditation

After a bit of practice with the above koans, choose a situation from your own life, whose outcome just cannot be predicted. It can be something as innocuous as "Will we win tonight's softball game?" or as serious as "Will I marry?" or "How long will I live?"

Focus your attention on the question, while trying to maintain a sense of "don't know" in your mind. Notice attempts to make rational predictions, "Our second baseman has the flu, but their best pitcher's arm is sore . . . ," but then gently return to the "don't know." Watch your mind as it vacillates between answer-seeking and "don't know."

Try to incorporate more "don't know" into your daily life. Will you catch that bus? Don't know. And that's okay. Will you get that raise? Don't know. And that's okay.

You can continue to strive wholeheartedly to catch the bus or get the raise, even *while* allowing it to be okay that you don't know whether it will happen or not. And—one last question, or perhaps I should say koan—will you make meditation an ongoing part of your life? Don't know. And that's okay, too.

Judging: The Double-Ended Sword

Minds just love to judge. Unfortunately, judging is a double-ended sword. And a double-ended sword has no safe place to grip. As you grab it, to swing at a real or imagined enemy, its razorlike handle cuts deeply into the flesh of your own hands.

"Judge not, lest ye be judged" is a statement that applies well to the mind. If we allow our minds to judge other people and events, our minds surely as boomerangs will turn around and judge us too. Quite literally, the sword that cuts both ways.

Learning not to judge so quickly has two great benefits. First, as we begin to relax the mind's judgment mode, we will judge ourselves less often, and less harshly. So the judging and the compassion exercises complement each other nicely.

Second, as we try to suspend our judgments of both thoughts and events, we find, as Carlos Castaneda's Don Juan put it, that everything becomes not *either* a blessing if we like it, or a curse if we don't, but a *challenge*. And our challenge is to try to use every thought, and every event of our life to take us in the direction of increasing enlightenment.

It's quite a task. Maybe, indeed, a full 100,000 mahacalpas' worth (see "How Long Should It Take," page 34). But the "Edge-

Pushing" and "Judging" exercises will help us get started, on a level that we can relate to, today.

The Thought-Judging Meditation

This simple little exercise is rather like the Thought-Labeling Exercise, only easier. Instead of watching each thought, and labeling each as to its category, just watch your passing thoughts and label each thought either as positive (you like the content of this thought), negative (you don't like the content of this thought), or neutral (no particular feelings toward this thought). If you find yourself getting *involved* with the specific content of the thought, as in "I really like Pontiacs—sure wish I had a Firebird—let's see, if I traded in the Hyundai . . ." gently note how you feel about getting caught up in content once again, and return to just noting: positive, negative, and neutral.

Noticing the constantly changing likes and dislikes of the mind without getting caught up in the emotions of liking or disliking will also help you to deal with actual events in the outside world as well. Instead of asking yourself "Do I like or dislike this event?" you'll begin to ask "How can I best meet this challenge in a way that will help me to go in whatever life direction that I choose?"

Since I hope that you are beginning to see the satisfaction of a more meditative, calmer, less judgmental way of life, you'll find, more and more often, that you prefer calm acceptance (which does *not* mean resignation, as I'll discuss later) to frenzied struggle, and compassionate understanding to anger. And whenever you "backslide," and yell or scream, or feel depressed, you'll be able to notice what you're doing, and gently, compassionately, return your mind to the way of the meditator.

The Acceptance Exercise

Choose something about yourself that you don't particularly like. It may be easier to begin with a physical rather than mental quality. I like to do this exercise in front of a mirror, and focus on the extra few pounds of flesh that stubbornly cling to my midsection, no matter how much I bike or kayak. Allow yourself, just for the three minutes of this exercise, to accept without judgment that which you don't like. Watch your mind. Is it resistant? Most likely it is, but the next exercises will help.

After doing this with a bodily focus, try accepting some un-likable element of your mind. I often use self-righteousness.

Now try to momentarily bring a feeling of acceptance to some external condition that you dislike. You might choose a social or political issue, or something about your job or life. Let it be okay for it to be exactly the way it is, just for three minutes.

Accepting these things doesn't mean that you won't try to change them in the near or distant future. It merely means that you are allowing them to exist right now, without self-hatred or judg-ment. Since they *do* exist, you are better off recognizing that and accepting them for right now.

Every act can be accomplished more effectively when our minds are unobscured by the clouds of judgment. Living with increased acceptance and decreased judgmentalness, we no longer need to use anger or self-hatred to motivate internal or external changes. We can simply *do* whatever seems to be most appropriate.

The Vicious Cycle:
Pain and Resistance

Imagine trying to push away a huge, thorny rosebush. The harder you push, the more its spines impale your hands. Pain often functions in this same, Catch-22 kind of manner, in which the more we resist it, the more it hurts. And the more it hurts, the more we attempt to resist it.

Learning to soften around pain, be it physical or mental, is difficult but rewarding. Often discomfort will diminish, or at least become more bearable, when we stop trying to push it away. We may even be able to realize, eventually, how our attempts to avoid pain actually help bring it right to us.

Pushing Our Limits

Of course it's hard not to resist pain. Although the top-of-the-line gurus seem virtually impervious to even terminal suffering, it's going to be a long haul before most of us can refrain from cursing a severely stubbed toe, a missed opportunity, or a tailgating truck driver.

So let's be realistic. Would a good boxing manager match his promising new kid, fresh from a local Golden Gloves triumph, against the reigning Olympic champ? He'd be nuts to do it, and he'd risk ruining his protégé. Instead, the manager would carefully match the young boxer against a series of challenging but not insurmountable opponents.

And when we begin to apply our new meditative skills to real-life challenges, we'll begin with small ones. We'll try to soften around the pain of a disappointing dinner, rather than the distress of a divorce. We'll practice forgiving the annoying bus driver, rather than an unscrupulous business competitor, or an abusive relative. We'll cultivate a Don't Know attitude on whether our friend will show up in time to make the eight o'clock movie, rather than on whether we get that new job we want so much.

Perhaps we'll try watching our thoughts as a moment of jealousy arises when a friend gets a compliment that we'd like for ourselves. Instead of the usual harsh judgment ("How can I possibly be jealous? He's my friend! What an awful person I am . . ."), maybe we can even observe that jealous thought with a touch of compassion. And then let go of that jealous thought, just for this moment.

Then maybe we'll be feeling anxious one day, but rather than immersing ourselves in the content of those fearful thoughts as usual, we'll merely practice a mind-clearing exercise for a few moments of relaxation and clarity.

Using the Three Minute Meditation exercises to work with these seemingly small challenges is actually of tremendous value. *Every* time we react in a meditative way instead of falling back on our habitual responses of judging, impatience, anger, or resistance—we push our edges, our limits, further out. Little by little, we develop the ability to live a compassionate and relaxed life, highly aware of our thoughts but not controlled by them.

Looking for the Truth Versus Protection of the Self-Image

One of the most important ways that we can push our limits is by trying to learn what is *true* about ourselves instead of trying to *protect* ourselves from pain. This would probably be considerably easier to do if the truth were always pleasant.

Unfortunately, many truths are painful to acknowledge. Some hurt because they contradict our ideas about what "a good person should be like." Others, whether positive or negative, because they contradict our ideas of what we ourselves are already like.

While we were growing up, we began to form a rather solid mental picture of who we were, or self-image. For most, this self-image becomes something that has to be maintained at all costs, whether appropriate or not.

For instance, I learned early on that boy children were supposed to be tough, and never cried. As a young adult, I was then forced to deny my feelings of fear or sadness, since they just didn't fit in with my self-image. I would fight when challenged by the local "hoods," or else experience terrible self-hatred because I had been "unmanly." I also had to deny my love for and dependence on my first long-term girlfriend, since neither emotion fit my "tough guy" image.

As another example, although I'd loved music as a child, when my voice changed during puberty I was ignominiously kicked out of the choir and told that "I just couldn't sing." Rather than face the pain and embarrassment that this caused me, I somehow decided that being tone-deaf (like my father thought he was) wasn't so bad. It seemed a tough, masculine, macho, trait.

I began to cut music class, and make fun of, even look down on, other kids who were members in the school band or orchestra. I absolutely ignored any evidence that I had been, or could be, a musical kind of guy.

After seven years of self-imposed "tone-deafness," during the late 1960s (the most pliable period of my life, up to then) I was able to buy a harmonica to take on a hitchhiking trip to Alaska. The fact that no one who picked me up knew me made it easier to go against my earlier unmusical self-image (however, a noticeable lack of virtuosity shortened many of my rides!).

The important part of this story is that for seven years I deprived myself of the joys of making music, because I was more interested in maintaining a particular facet of my self-image, than in looking for and learning about what was true.

Truth and Self-Protection in Relationships

This conflict between truth and self-protection is an unusually efficient producer of pain in our relationships with others. In my old relationships to family and lovers, I would invariably become angry rather than face even the slightest feelings of rejection. Of course, getting mad then increased the distance between us (usually resulting in even more feelings of rejection and thus more anger). Once I became able to notice my thoughts of rejection, and experience the pain of them, I then often became able to either console myself with a compassion exercise or share my feelings with the other person.

I strongly recommend the book *Do I Have to Give Up Me to Be Loved By You?* (written by two therapists, Jordan and Margaret Paul—now, ironically, divorced—and published by CompCare) for anyone who'd like to work with issues of truth versus self-protection in the context of a relationship.

Simple Pain/Resistance Exercises

These exercises simply involve observing pain as just another focus for meditation. As we observe the pain sensations, we'll try to "soften" around them, instead of tightening around them as we usually do.

Since it's almost impossible to tighten around severe pain without lots of practice, these exercises begin with moderate and self-controlled doses of discomfort. And remember, these exercises are not to be performed competitively, with much gritting of teeth, but with gentleness and compassion. If you find yourself trying to "tough these out," perhaps you'd better return to the section on compassion for a while.

The Hot Pepper Meditation

I like spicy food. Even so, I often reach a point in which I am "hotted out." My mouth and lips burn, and I wish that I hadn't overindulged. Although overuse of hot sauce or chili peppers can be momentarily unpleasant, it is not physically harmful, and of short duration. So it is a good way to practice softening against pain.

If you aren't a fan of hot food, be careful. Even one drop of Tabasco™ or other hot condiments may give you more of a reaction than you've bargained for! Remember, these are not endurance exercises!

Spend a moment doing your favorite mind-clearing exercise, and then eat an amount of hot sauce that's a bit more than you'd usually use. Try to focus on the sensation of pain, just as you've focused on so many other objects of meditation.

Observe your thoughts. Do you want to rush for a glass of ice water, yell at the waiter, be angry at me, or yourself ("What a dumb exercise!"), or cry? Does your body or jaw tense up? Your eyes tear? Your preferred thought, right now, is simply to *investigate* how you react to pain.

Try to relax, to soften around the sensations in your mouth. Even as your lips are burning, do a quick relaxation exercise, or mind clearer. After the hotness recedes, try again. See if you can push your limits while maintaining a clear, focused mind.

The Cold Shower Meditation

You can perform a similar meditation while showering. Just make the water a bit colder than you normally prefer, while doing one of the mind-clearing or relaxation meditations. Once again, be compassionate. Compassion in this context means doing the exercise, and pushing your limits, only to the extent that you can do so without being self-punishing.

Some people like to do this exercise using both slightly hotter- and colder-than-normal water (ask your doctor about this if you are under a physician's care, and don't burn yourself). Just gradually change the shower setting from a bit too hot to a bit too cold, while meditating and trying not to tighten up, either mentally or physically. This gently approximates the experience of the Native American sweat lodge, in which the participants alternate between hovering over steaming rocks in an enclosed shelter, and jumping into an ice-cold river.

Going back and forth between too hot and too cold can help remind us that we can stay centered within our minds, no matter what is happening on the outside. It's too hot now, in the sweat lodge? Soon it will be too cold, in the river. Then too hot again. . . .

Other Pain/Resistance Exercises

After you've experimented with these self-controlled pain/resistance meditations, try softening around minor pains that you *cannot* control. I use a neighbor's barking dog for a meditation focus sometimes. Although listening to the dog's incessant barking can be annoying, when I just focus on the sound, the physical sensation, of each bark without thinking, "He shouldn't bark" or, "Why isn't it more quiet"—the noise doesn't bother me anymore . . . By shifting my focus, the dog has, once again, become my teacher instead of my tormentor.

I find that I can sometimes do the same with headaches and backaches as well, or minor disappointments, just by consciously softening around them. When in pain, instead of gritting my teeth and tightening my muscles, I may consciously try to relax my stomach, my jaw, my back, my neck. Perhaps I'll do a relaxation exercise, as on page 99. Maybe I'll even try to do visualizations of sending some love and compassion directly into the place that's hurting.

In times of mental pain or disappointment, instead of tightening my mind up, and feeling fearful, angry, or somehow blaming myself, I may try a Compassion exercise, coupled with some thought watching. Perhaps I'll soothe myself by thinking about the Master Skill (page 129). And occasionally I still yell, and complain, and reach for the aspirin bottle! But a healthy dose of compassion helps me to recognize and accept that I handled the pain as best I could at that exact moment in my life.

Of course, the bigger the pain, mental or physical, the more practice and effort it takes to soften around it. That's why it's wise not to wait until you're desperate to start working on these important skills.

If you suffer from ongoing physical pain, or are interested in pursuing this type of meditation in greater depth, Stephen Levine devotes careful attention to working with pain in *Who Dies*. Once again, I cannot recommend his book too highly! My own week-long meditation workshop with Stephen was a turning point in my life, and teaching him to play the blues harmonica a great privilege!

I Am

Many meditators call exercises based on the following concept "the high road without rails." It is probably the most metaphysically sophisticated and least intuitively obvious style of meditation around. So read about it, think about it if you like, try it if you dare. Then, if it seems interesting, get the Sri Nisargadatta book listed in the bibliography. It's one of my two or three favorite books—I've read it a dozen times, and occasionally even think I understand a paragraph or two! Another favorite book which tackles this subject, and a much easier read besides, is Stephen Levine's often-mentioned *Who Dies*.

Consider the statements "I am happy," or "I am tired," or "I am bored." They are all statements of temporary validity. No one is ever permanently happy, or tired, or bored. At other times, we can also validly make the negative statement "I am not happy," or "I am not tired," or "I am not bored."

But no one can ever truthfully make just the statement "I am not," or "I do not exist." As long as a person exists enough to say or think "I am," they just cannot honestly say, or think, "I am not." So one part of each statement—happy or not, bored or not—is permanently true: the *"I am."*

Although your physical body and your intellectual makeup have probably changed significantly since you were a baby, this basic sense of "I am" remains remarkably stable. Think back to an early childhood memory. The six-year-old that you were had a clear sense of "I am." You could confidently state, "I *am* a first-grader" or "I *am* a good reader." Your child's sense of "I am" was and is the same as your sense of "I am" right now, as you think, "I *am* a Three Minute Meditator" or "I *am* hungry."

Yet it's hard to describe the "I am" feeling, although we use it as an expression dozens of times each day. Perhaps it is easiest to identify this sensation when we awaken in the morning. Just exactly as our eyes first open, before we know where, or even who, we are—there is always a sense of (for want of a better word) "am-ness." Someone, or something, some awareness or consciousness, appears to be in the body, looking out. And this "I am" feeling is always present, unless we are in a state of dreamless sleep. In some traditions, this sense of "I am" is called "the witness."

This sense of existing, this sense of "am-ness" that all people possess, is the basis for a series of the most subtle and difficult but important meditations. They are important because the "I am" is, in a very real way, the connection between the small mind of the individual and the big mind of God, or the universal consciousness.

According to the Meditator's worldview, the "I am" sense in your individual mind is a very small piece of consciousness that is a part of *all* consciousness, just as a tiny bay is a small, connected, part of the entire ocean. Unfortunately, we usually don't focus our attention on the "I am" feeling clearly enough to realize and perceive the connection. Our minds are too busy with the day-to-day problems and gratifications of the workaday world. We constantly focus on "I am hungry," or "I am a smart person," but never just on the "I am."

An analogy: On a windless summer night the full moon is perfectly mirrored in the still waters of the pond. But agitate the water, and the moon's tiny reflection is jumbled, broken, perhaps unrecognizable.

Eventually, as your mind begins to quiet through meditation, the agitations of thought—desires, fears, thoughts of past and future, the "I am hungry" and "I am a good golfer"—become still and quiet for short periods of time. Then, like the moon, a reflection of the universal consciousness of the Meditator's worldview begins to shine in the "I am" of your clear mental waters. Amazingly, you don't even have to believe in this, for it to happen. You just have to do it.

The "I Am Happy," "I Am Sad" Meditation

Relax for a moment with a mind-clearing meditation, and then choose two contradictory "I am" statements, like "I am happy" and "I am sad," or "I am tired" and "I am alert."

Take one, and visualize it as clearly as possible. If you chose "I am tired," picture yourself yawning, and feel the sluggishness of your body. Then quickly visualize the other one, "I am alert." Picture yourself brimming with vigor, feeling energetic, eyes bright and watchful. Go back and forth between the two, and try to feel how neither is very "true."

Now just say "I am" to yourself, sink deep into the sense of "I am," and experience how "true" that seems. Try to observe the sensation "I am." What is it like? Is some one or some thing, some awareness, inside you, looking out? Who? Who am I?

The "Who Am I?" Meditation

After a moment of mind clearing, ask yourself the question "Who am I?" "Who am I *really*?" Are you your name? Your memory? Your reputation? None of these will probably seem to be you, since you can live perfectly well without any of them.

Are you your body? Perhaps, but your body can continue to exist without a mind in it. If that happened, would your mindless body still be you? You *have* a body, but your body is not you.

Ask yourself "Who asks the question, 'Who am I?'" Or even ask yourself the question: "Who asks the question: "Who asks the question, 'Who am I?'"" Hello? Anybody home? Someone must be, to be asking all these questions.

This exercise can function as a koan, a Don't Know meditation. Or perhaps, like many who have asked it, you will return to the Meditator's worldview, and conclude that the "I" of "Who am

I?" is a piece of "recycled" consciousness, which *animates* the body that it inhabits—the "witness" of so many meditative traditions, a little bit of God.

If you like this exercise, practice it anytime, by asking questions such as "Who desires?" and "Who fears?" whenever you notice a thought arising. Who thinks? And do read Sri Nisargadatta's *I Am That*. It's difficult, but rewarding.

Impermanence

It's a cliché, once again, but true: *Nothing* is permanent except for the fact that everything changes. Everything that you think you know about yourself, your body, your job, your loved ones, your country will alter with the passage of time.

Much of the pain that we experience in our lives comes from the desire to hold on to what must inevitably change. We hurt when our parents grow old and die, and we hurt when our children grow up and move away. We hurt when we lose the strength or beauty of our youth, or the prestige that our work brings us.

If our desire for protection from pain supersedes our desire to face what is true, we are doomed to live lives that attempt to limit or ignore change. And that's sure to hurt. Lots. Of course, facing change will bring pain also. But each meditative step that we take will lessen the amount of pain that we must experience when we face and accept change and impermanence.

This exercise is based on the work of Stephen Levine, one of many teachers (including Don Juan, Ram Dass, Alan Watts, and Elizabeth Kubler-Ross) who stress using the knowledge of mortality to add vitality to life. If you find this concept interesting, read any of their books, as listed in the bibliography. John White's *A*

Practical Guide to Death and Dying also has many exercises and meditations on this subject.

Stephen tells a story of a wise man who was given a beautiful and delicate goblet. It was knocked over, and broke, but the wise man only smiled. "Even" he said, "as I held it to the light and admired it, it was already broken in my mind . . ."

Every sensation we feel, every relationship we have, is made more real and poignant by the advance knowledge of its transitory nature. And how can we fail to develop a sense of compassion and camaraderie towards any being that must exist in this fragile and transient environment that we call life?

The Horn Has Already Honked

The car approaches an intersection where the traffic light is yellow or red. Instruct your driver not to move the car until the car behind you honks its horn.

Relax the muscles of your body, and focus your mind on the inexorability of that honking horn. It's going to honk, a rude, abrupt, noise. There is absolutely nothing that you can do to control the situation, except to accept the inevitable, and possibly by doing so reduce your own impulse to jump or be startled.

Soften your mind around that impending honk. Witness your own tension, witness your resistance to this exercise. It's a hard one to do, because it goes against everything you've ever been taught. Observe your desire to tighten mind and body against the honk, and watch your desire to make judgments, like "This is a stupid exercise," or "What an impatient jerk the driver behind me is!" And perhaps also look at your own desire to somehow avoid the unavoidable.

More on Death and Dying

So many changes in life are inevitable. Death, old age, loss. Yet rather than accepting these as a natural part of life, we complain about them, we tighten against them, and we deny their existence.

The death of self or loved ones is perhaps the biggest, yet most inevitable, change. Every person now alive will be dead within ten, fifty, or a hundred years. It's difficult, and excruciat-ingly painful, to face what I call the "Devil's Contract": that we will all be forced to experience the death of everyone that we love, or else they will be forced to experience ours. There is no other alternative. And no easy answer.

Dealing with the knowledge of one's own unavoidable death is the ultimate level of choosing truth over protection of self-image. It is neither a simple nor an easy thing to do. But meditation, and especially compassion, can help.

In my counseling work with grieving and terminally ill adults and children, I've found all of the meditative techniques described in this book to be valuable, both for me, in my counseling work and my life, and for those clients willing to try them.

Freedom

We generally think of freedom as the ability to do whatever we want. But this type of "freedom" will always be limited, as no one can ever completely control their world. Even kings and rock stars must contend with accidents, disease, aging, pain, and other people, not to mention their own fears and desires.

True freedom lies rather in the ability to allow whatever is happening, moment by changing moment, to be all right. Without judging or resistance, and with compassion for both self and others. Using every thought and event as a meditation lesson, a challenge (neither curse nor blessing). Building a road towards enlightenment out of the very rocks and obstacles that appear to block our way.

Actions Versus Outcomes

Allowing "whatever happens to be all right" does not imply passivity. We can work with zest and enthusiasm towards any goal that we decide on, or struggle powerfully to oppose that which we believe to be wrong. However, even though we direct all our energy into *actions* aimed at a particular goal, we can try to remain unattached to the eventual *outcome* or *result* of our actions. Experiment with this. Make dinner from a new recipe. Do so carefully, but without worrying about how it comes out.

Whenever we make our happiness dependent upon specific results, we inevitably invite pain. Because although we can take responsibility for our actions, the results of our actions, the fruits of our labor, can *never* be controlled.

For example, Mahatma Gandhi's work towards India's freedom from Britain was intensely motivated and powerfully executed. But didn't this same work eventually "result" in the Bangladeshi war and famine that killed millions? Einstein's theoretical breakthroughs were instrumental in ending World War II. But now the fruits of his labor threaten to begin and end World War III, and everything else, as well.

Recalling the Meditator's view of cause and effect (page 29) may help us to realize that actions and outcomes are not as clearly or directly related as we are sometimes tempted to think. How can we possibly expect to control anything as complex and interrelated as this crazy, mysterious world that we exist in?

The Master Skill

In our busy and status-conscious culture, it's easy to place a great deal of importance on things that happen. We judge ourselves by what we own or don't own, by what we accomplish or don't accomplish. We forget that how we *respond* to whatever happens is more important, in the long run, than the particular event that happens.

Meditation teaches us that how we respond or react to our thoughts is more important than the thoughts themselves. We learn to watch the process of the mind, instead of getting caught up in the content of each thought that passes through. Similarly, we begin to see that the process of learning to deal skillfully with *whatever* occurs is far more important than attempting (futilely, of course) to control the outcome or content of each particular incident in our lives.

We all possess a variety of skills to one degree or another. There are verbal skills and athletic skills, business skills and popularity skills. But there is one skill that's more worth cultivating than all the rest combined.

If we practice living in the Now, with awareness of and compassion for our daily fears and desires, we can deal powerfully and effectively with whatever happens in our lives. Even painful

This Master Skill is the skill of being able to use the Three Minute Meditation techniques in real-life situations. It is more important than any specific event, no matter how important that particular event may seem. In a very real way, it is more important to be able to lose the race, or the job, or the relationship and still feel okay, than it would be to win that race, that job, that man or woman. Because eventually there will be a race that we can't win, or a relationship that must end.

thoughts, even unpleasant events, can be used to remind us of the meditative work that is our most real and important job on this earth. In this way we can turn *all* that happens, painful or pleasant, into grist for our meditative mill.

The Master Skill Visualization Exercise

Read the above section carefully. Think about it. *Feel* how true it is. Then, using the techniques described in the meditation visualization section (page 95), picture yourself involved in a situation in which the outcome is most definitely *not* what you had wished for. You didn't get the raise, or the job, or the trip to Hawaii.

Picture yourself *using* the skills and knowledge that you are gaining from this book, including the specific exercises or techniques that you might use, to handle the situation with calmness, acceptance, and compassion. This is the Master Skill.

Part III

Using the Three Minute Meditations

If you've made it this far in the book, you've already read about a wide variety of meditation techniques. I hope that you've been *doing* them, as well—because your success at applying these exercises to real-life situations is likely to depend on how much you've practiced them.

Of course, as I've already explained, in my kayaking and karate analogies, we can apply our skills to a wide range of situations. And the more extreme the situation, the better shape we need to be in to deal skillfully with it. Even a beginning aikido practitioner may be able to gently and gracefully disarm a small, weak aggressor who's armed with a plastic fork. But it might take a high-degree black belt, one in perfect shape and trained to the minute, to successfully deal with a trio of knife-wielding muggers. Using a breath-counting meditation to soften around the anger you feel when the guy who cuts you off on the highway then "flips you the bird" may require far less training than using the exercise to soften around the anger you feel when the boss gives *your* promotion to that new coworker.

If we always knew exactly what the future held for us, we could wait until we knew that a tough time was coming up, then frantically spend a few weeks in spiritual training for it. And sometimes we can make special preparations in advance of special events. But the world is a funny, unpredictable place. We never really know just what's going to happen, and that's why it's so important to *stay* in shape, as the following examples from my life demonstrate.

Practice Doesn't Make Perfect, but It Helps

As my daughter's birth approached in late 1988, I went into serious "mental training" for the event. For nearly two months I meditated as much as possible, doing both long (for me) fifteen minute morning meditations and lots of short ones (three seconds to three minutes long) throughout the day. The labor was long, but thirty hours into it I was still in relatively alert and relaxed shape. When I went down to the hospital cafeteria for a sandwich and discovered in the morning newspaper a long and rather flattering article on the local publisher who had a few years before "appropriated" the concept of my harmonica book, it scarcely unbalanced me. Before I had begun meditating, a single thought of this publisher could easily consume my mind for hours, if not days. But because I was metaphysically in good shape, I was able to see the humor in the situation ("Ah yes—a quick quiz from the cosmic consciousness, to see if I'm in good mental control—un huh!"), and put it out of my mind in order to attend to the labor at hand.

Contrastingly, in late 1989 I was feeling somewhat smug. The sequel to this book, *MetaPhysical Fitness*, had just gone to the printers. I was loving fatherhood, and busy with a variety of projects that promised to be quite successful. My diligence at meditation, even Three Minute Meditation, hit a low. So when some fairly serious business disappointments struck without warning, I was unable at first to work with the feelings of pain, anger, resistance, and fear that arose. I was a miserable mess for a few days. Then, fortunately, the *pain itself* reminded me to make my own meditation practice a priority once again. Soon I was able to place my work problems in perspective and deal with them diligently, but without excessive attachments to end results. This was possible because I knew that I had a set of mental tools to use—even though I had become spiritually kind of flabby and out of shape! Perhaps this unpleasant experience will remind me to try to stay in decent spiritual shape—at least, I hope so!

Working with the Problem Areas

In each of the following eight problem areas—Tension, Anger, Self-Acceptance, Fears and Phobias, Loss and Grief, Feelings of Loneliness and Emptiness, Control Issues, and Codependency—we'll be using at least three of the techniques from Part Two. We'll combine the practice of softening around pain (first described on page 113) with the meditation visualization (page 96). We'll also practice remembering the importance of the Master Skill—and merely remembering the Master Skill (page 129) is the first step towards mastering it.

You'll probably notice that the instructions on dealing with these six seemingly very different problem areas are surprisingly similar. That's because the problems are all caused by thoughts in the mind—and all thoughts, although their contents may differ—can be worked with in the same way.

A Brief Note on the Difference (or Lack Thereof) Between Thoughts and Feelings

In the following sections, I'll be talking a lot about strong feelings or emotions like anger, fear, judgment, and grief. It's going to be important (for you and me both) to remember the main difference between thoughts and feelings or emotions.

What's the difference? Well, thoughts are the mental images that pop up into our minds. Feelings or emotions occur when we react to these thoughts. So feelings are simply our reactions to thoughts that we are very caught up in, that we identify ourselves with.

Let's say that a friend has disappointed us. When we say to ourselves "I am angry," or even "I feel angry," it means that we are letting a moment of angry thought define us completely—we are relating or reacting *from* our mind. If we say instead "I am having an angry thought," we are relating *to* our mind. Rather than being totally caught up in (or *reacting* to) the content of the mind, we are observing the process of (or *relating* to) the mind. If this seems confusing, please reread pages 37-38. Much of our work in the following sections will involve learning to identify the thoughts that we get caught up in, the thoughts that we have strong reactions to, and discovering ways to work with them more skillfully. The more we meditate, the more we are able to react to any thought, no matter how powerful or disturbing, with calm acceptance and compassion rather than fear, denial, or anger.

What Is . . . ?

You'll notice that each of the following sections begins with a question: "What Is Tension?" or: "What Is Anger?" Before we can work with a problem area, we must be able to look at it with honesty and clarity. And that's sometimes not easy, even with things that aren't problem areas! For instance, as discussed in the Eating Meditation on page 91, how many of us usually notice subtleties such as the fact that pea skins taste differently from pea insides? And if we can barely observe *peas* with mindfulness, with nonjudgmental awareness, how can we expect to really observe anger, or fear, or loneliness?

These "What Is . . ." questions don't attempt to describe tension, or anger, or fear. Rather, they are meant to inspire you to dig beneath the commonly used but rarely understood word names and experience the thoughts themselves, directly.

More than Half the Battle

Learning to experience these painful and difficult sensations and situations with mindfulness—that is, without denial, and without judgment—isn't easy. That's precisely why we begin our practice by focusing attention on our breath, our steps, on the peas we eat instead of on our anger or our fear. But once we learn to experience even our unpleasant feelings without avoidance, we'll become able to understand them, and to apply a variety of meditation techniques to our thoughts about them. In fact, learning to look at the workings of the mind with the compassion of the heart is much more than half the battle—it's usually the end of the battle!

What to Do When You Blow It

Of course you'll blow it—big surprise! These six topics include the knottiest problems that a human being can face, so expecting ourselves to deal perfectly with them is just another excuse for judging ourselves harshly. But instead of judging when we do blow it—and get tense, or angry, or fearful, or grief-stricken—we can learn to *use* our mistakes.

Professional athletes watch videos of their games, and often observe their mistakes even more carefully than their successes. That's an important technique for improving their playing. Likewise, by carefully observing how, when, and why we blow it, we can learn how *not* to blow it quite so often, or so enthusiastically. Using our mistakes to learn from is what Stephen Levine calls "turning manure into fertilizer," because we can gain something incredibly valuable if we choose to do so, instead of grabbing yet another opportunity for self-judging and self-hate. And it's the clear, judgment-free observation, the looking for the truth with mindful clarity, that allows us to do this.

Once we've learned to apply meditation techniques after the fact, we can begin to apply them *during* thoughts of anger, or fear, or grief. And eventually, we can use meditation preventively, to help prepare ourselves to deal with those potential "blow it" situations.

Choosing a Favorite Mini-Meditation

For me, choosing one or two particular meditations and practicing them as much as possible has been of tremendous value, even though at times I also enjoy using a wider variety of techniques. But over the past few years I've found that the breath-counting (page 72) and the step-counting exercises (page 73) are the ones that I can do virtually anytime, anywhere.

I do dozens of breath-counting meditations every day. Some last for only one or two breaths at a time. One of my favorites is the One-Breath Compassion Meditation, based on the Heartgill Meditation on page 101. I just breathe a big, sighing breath of compassion right into my heart, and breathe out (again with a sigh) any pain that remains. Whenever I remember (at least a few times a day), I throw in a Chore-Based Breath Count (see page 73) during some mindless chore.

I also do a dozen or so Step-Counting Meditations every day during the few steps it takes to walk from my desk to the bathroom. Feel free to do longer ones, but I find that it's the "minis" that are most often appropriate for use in the midst of the hubbub of daily life.

Having a few really solid "old standbys" will be extremely helpful in the following applications, simply by facilitating the mindful attention that is so crucial to the use of meditation in real life. If my favorites don't appeal to you, try to become *very* familiar with the one or two exercises that feel best, plus a short compassion meditation. Practice them often (at least five or ten times a day), but in tiny doses. From now on, I'll sometimes invite you to "use your favorite" for a moment or two. Why don't you do just that, right now, then go on, refreshed, to the next section!

Tension (and Relaxation)

What Is Tension?

When we use the word "tension," and its opposite, "relaxation," we are most often referring to the physical sensation of tightness, or its absence, in the muscular system of the body. You've already (I hope) practiced the "warm and heavy" technique on page 99, which will help you to relax your body. Tension has a mental component as well, and by looking closely at the sensation of tension, it's possible to gain a much more subtle understanding of both the mental and physical elements that result in the experience of this less than pleasant sensation. The following exercise will help, especially if you've already worked with page 99.

The Body Scan Meditation

You've already learned to focus your attention on your breath and on your feet, on a candle flame and on your peas. In this exercise, move the focus of your attention in a slow *scan* of your entire body, from head to foot.

Look for tense areas as you scan. I tend to tighten and raise my left shoulder towards my neck and head, and sometimes clench my stomach muscles. Where do you tend to experience tension?

In this exercise, unlike the previous "warm and heavy" exercise, you aren't trying to relax tight spots, you're simply attempting to experience them. So don't wait until you're relaxed to do this one—spring it on yourself, as a "flash quiz" on the subject of your tension! After you do this one a few times, you may begin to identify tense spots that you don't usually notice (you probably didn't need this exercise to locate your obvious trouble spots).

When you identify a tense neck or jaw (lots of us hold tension in the face, brow, mouth, or even behind the eyes), do a few seconds of your favorite mini-meditation. Then ask yourself: What does it feel like here? Is it painful? Dull pain or sharp? Is there a hot feeling? Is there anxiety or some other emotion present as you observe the tension spot?

Tension and Anxiety

When I look carefully at any tension area in my body, I find that the physical tension is often accompanied by a feeling of mild, generalized fearfulness. This type of sensation, which psychologists usually call "free-floating anxiety," seems to me to have two main causes, one more physically based, and the other more mentally based.

On the physical level, tightness of the stomach muscles always results in shallow breathing. Shallow breathing is likely to result in hyperventilation, which occurs when you try to compensate for the shallowness of the breath by taking faster breaths. As you breathe faster, the oxygen level in your bloodstream rises and the carbon dioxide level drops. This sets off a chain reaction in your body which makes it difficult to catch your breath at all. And difficulty in breathing is enough to produce a panic attack in almost anyone—especially if you don't understand what is going on physically. A number of the people suffering from acute "acid freakouts" that I've worked with were actually suffering from undiagnosed hyperventilation, and just needed help relaxing, and breathing more slowly and deeply! The following exercise will help you to do just that.

On the mental level, hidden or unexplored thoughts often cause the muscular tightening that we experience as tension. By bringing these thoughts into the open and working with them, we can begin to eliminate these tension makers with the Tension-Thought Labeling/Softening Meditation.

✦ The Stomach-Softening Meditation

Sit quietly, and do a minute of your favorite meditation. Then focus your attention onto your belly—any tension there? Let the muscles be loose, without making any attempt to keep your stomach pulled in (as so many of us unconsciously do).

Now place both palms gently on your belly. Imagine that your hands are coated with glue, and slowly pull them outward as you inhale, so that your stomach (not chest) expands to the fullest comfortable position. When ready to inhale, just let your hands follow your stomach back in. No thinking, no judging, just breathing deep into that soft stomach.

While doing this, you can either do a breath-labeling meditation (in . . . out . . .), a breath-counting exercise, or a breath experiencing. Try to stay focused on the stomach, and if any thoughts arise, as usual, return to the meditation as soon as you notice you've wandered.

Tension Thought Labeling/Softening Meditation

This exercise, as you may have guessed from the name, is a variation of the Thought-Labeling Meditation (page 85). Throughout the day, attempt to notice feelings of tension whenever you can. If it seems difficult to spontaneously recognize tension, do a very quick Body Scan as often as you think of it. If you identify tension, do a moment of experiencing thoughts (page 87) and see if there are any thoughts of fear, anger, or judgment (or other painful thoughts) lurking beneath the tension.

If you can identify such a thought, do a moment of your favorite meditation (or the soft-stomach breath) while you hold the thought in your mind, and see if you can soften around the pain of the thought. I'll discuss softening around mental pain in more detail in the section on Fears and Phobias, and you may wish to reread the Pain and Resistance section on page 117 as well.

The Relaxation Visualization Exercise

You'll find it well worthwhile to spend one or two minutes a day visualizing yourself using the above (and below) exercises. Simply picture yourself feeling tense, in a situation that usually causes you to feel that way. You may want to "artificially" tighten up, to make the visualization more realistic, and bring a common tension-causing thought into your mind. Then, as you relax, picture yourself doing a few stomach-softening breaths, and also softening around the pain of the tension-causing thought. You'll also want to do this exercise with the "Relaxation Button" technique, below.

Stress Buttons, Relaxation Buttons

Most of us have had the experience of knowing someone who could "really push our buttons." So we're quite aware of the existence of "stress buttons." What many of us don't realize is that just as the fight-or-flight response has its opposite in the relaxation response (page 13), "relaxation buttons" can work just as effectively as "stress buttons"!

To create a relaxation button, simply practice using a *very* brief relaxation breathing technique. Use one that requires only a single breath, and pair it in your mind with some particular daily event, as described below. Perhaps you can do a labeling or experiencing meditation for one breath, or do a single stomach softening breath. Perhaps you'll want to try an adaptation of the Ahhh/Oooh Meditation (page 102), in which you'll breathe in tension, and breathe out relaxation.

Punching the Relax Button

Choose whichever breathing meditation you like. Do it often in the course of your daily routine, and also practice imagining its use a few times a day with the Relaxation Visualization Exercise above. I often like to tie the use of my relaxation button (for me, usually a single labeled breath) to using the copy machine, something I do many times each day. I just make a habit of hitting my relax button every time I hit the copy button! On especially stressful days, I may even turn on the hour alarm of my watch, and hit my relaxation button every time I hear the little chime, no matter what else I'm doing.

Of course, many times you won't remember to punch the relax button until after you've become tense or anxious. But the more often you use it, the better you will become at identifying the situations in which you need to use it, and soon you'll find yourself pushing the relaxation button "preventively"—that is, before you even need it!

Relaxation and the Master Skill

As I've said before, the ability to use the Three Minute Meditation Method in daily life is more important than having events in your life happen as you want them to. So it really makes sense to make the time to create relaxation buttons that will work for you, no matter how busy you are or how many other things you seem to need to do first. By focusing on this priority, you'll create a tool that will be of tremendous value in everything you do.

Anger

What Is Anger?

Anger is one of those types of thoughts that we all experience, but rarely look at clearly. In fact, most of us usually don't think of anger as a thought, but consider it an emotion or feeling. However, by learning to say "I'm having angry thoughts" rather than "I am angry," we place anger more under our own control, instead of letting it control us. If angry thoughts often (or even occasionally) bring you pain, this section may be helpful.

The Anger-Labeling Exercise

Watching the mind has been our main method of learning to relate to our thoughts as objects for our attention (rather than relating to our thoughts as though they *were* us). And one of the simplest mind-watching exercises is the Particular Thought-Counting Meditation (page 86).

In this variation of that meditation, you don't even need to bother to count the number of times anger arises during a day (unless you want to—I usually find it discouraging!). Just agree with yourself to try to notice and label any type of angry thought that comes into your mind. Label the thought by silently saying something like "Ah yes, there's anger, all right." No need to judge the thought, or analyze it, or try to change it. Just label it, *as soon as you've identified it* (promptness is important, here). If the thought stays in your mind, and you choose to dwell on it and "be angry," that's okay for now.

Do this exercise at least three times, each one for long enough so that you have a few opportunities to notice and label an angry thought. This may mean "programming" yourself to label angry thoughts for anywhere from half an hour to a week, depending on how often you tend to get angry. Once you've learned to identify angry thoughts quickly whenever they occur, you'll be ready for the next meditation. If angry thoughts are difficult for you to identify, you may want to skip this exercise and instead begin with the next one.

The Experiencing Anger Meditation: Practice

Prepare for this meditation by bringing clearly into your mind something that usually "makes you angry." It might be an image of a person or situation, or a memory of some past irritation. What does it feel like to have the angry thought in your mind? Is all or part of your body tense? Does your breathing feel different— faster, or more shallow? Are you able to watch the angry thought, instead of getting caught up in it's content?

When an angry thought enters my mind, I often find (if I can observe it rather than just "get mad") that my jaw tenses, my eyes squint, and my breathing gets fast and shallow. I also find, when I try to observe anger, that my mind is full of reasons why the angry thought is both important and justifiable (and thus why I should act on it, and yell or feel even angrier, rather than try to experience it).

I usually find that alternating a few seconds of experiencing the anger as clearly as possible with a few seconds of my favorite mind-clearing meditation is the best way to look at anger without getting caught up in it. The mind-clearing break, though short, helps me to sit back and "watch the movie."

Practice visualizing yourself using meditation to soften around angry thoughts, using the above alternation of experiencing the anger and doing your favorite meditation. The more you do this, the easier it will be to soften around the anger thoughts that arise in real life situations, instead of reacting to them in the usual unskillful ways.

The Experiencing Anger Meditation: In Real Life

Of course, purposely creating an angry thought and then observing it is often different than having one enter your mind unbidden. So after you've done the practice Experiencing Anger Meditation at least once or twice (or whenever you feel ready), go back to the Anger-Labeling Exercise. But this time, instead of just labeling the first actual angry thought that enters your mind, take a moment to experience the sensations that come with the angry thought as soon as you've labeled it. Do these sensations seem different than the ones you experienced with the "practice" angry thought? Less controllable, perhaps? Big surprise?

Please spend some time observing anger before attempting to work with it, as described in the following sections. And try not to judge yourself for having angry thoughts. Becoming angry with yourself for being angry only trains you to have more angry thoughts. It's pretty natural, of course, but not very useful! So try not to be judgmental—after all, you're working on it, so give yourself a break!

Anger and Thought Chains

After beginning to learn to experience anger on a level of mostly physical sensation, as above, you can start to analyze the thought process that leads to anger thoughts. Reread the "Rube Goldberg" Thought-Chain Meditation on page 86, then begin looking for the thoughts (or the incidents that bring up the thoughts) that precede your angry thoughts.

As I've said, angry thoughts are often the result of thoughts of fear and helplessness. And I have recently begun to realize that many of my anger thoughts arise from a particularly type of judging thought, which I label "resentment." For me, resentment means making a negative judgment about the way things are because of my underlying and usually unexplored belief that the universe is supposed to treat me in a certain way (with kid gloves). So, since at some deep level I expect everything to be easy and painless, when events don't match my expectations, I get mad! But by bringing this hidden belief into conscious view, I realize its fallacy, and can let go of the resentful thought sooner.

Working with Anger

Becoming aware of the thought chains that lead to anger will, with practice, give you a second or two of warning before the angry thought can get a good foothold in your mind. You can then begin to try softening around the anger *as soon as you identify it*. For some of you, nothing more complicated than a moment of your favorite meditation will be necessary (although disciplining yourself to do it at the appropriate time isn't always easy). Others may find the Heartgill or Ahhh/Oooh Meditations (pages 101-102) helpful. The Simple Pain/Resistance Exercises (page 116) provide good preliminary practice for working with anger, as most of us find hot peppers or cold water much more manageable than rage, or even well-justified irritation!

Repressing Anger?

Please remember: You are not trying to avoid having any angry thoughts at all. You are simply trying not to get caught up in them, trying not to react angrily to them. When you can *look at* anger without *getting* angry (at your either yourself for having them or at the object of your thoughts), anger is no longer a problem. It's just one of the many thoughts that pass through the mind.

I'm not saying that this is easy to do—anger is one of my grabbier thoughts. Whenever I find myself *reacting* to my anger thoughts, rather than *relating* to them, I'm unpleasantly reminded of Groucho Marx in the classic *Duck Soup*, in which Groucho is president of some mythical country. After having been insulted by the ambassador of a neighboring country, Groucho has graciously buried the hatchet. Buried it so far, indeed, that he cannot even remember the original insult. As he laughingly tries to bring it to mind while chatting pleasantly with the ambassador, he goes from the *process of* discussing the insult, to getting caught up in his reaction to the *content* of the insult itself. And, of course, he gets madder and madder, until war is declared!

If other meditations don't seem to allow you to relate to, rather than from, your angry thoughts while in the midst of them, you may find that doing any short version of the Compassion Meditations will help. Or try my One-Breath Compassion Exercise (page 136). If you encountered a small child that you love in a state of pain and anger, you'd hug the child, and offer love and compassion. So even though you feel angry, judgmental, or resentful, there is no reason not to offer yourself compassion. In fact, when you're experiencing these painful emotions, that's exactly when you need compassion the most!

Anger and the Master Skill

Anger does have its rewards. Expression of our angry feelings may help us to get our way, and self-righteous anger can be quite satisfying. Remembering the Master Skill, however, can help us in two ways. It can remind us of the bigger satisfaction that we attain by dealing meditatively with difficult thoughts and situations, rather than letting our anger control us. And it can remind us to treat ourselves skillfully, and with compassion, even when we experience thoughts that we'd rather avoid—reminding us that learning how to work with our anger is more useful than never being angry at all.

Self-Acceptance

What Is Self-Acceptance?

Although most of us have lots of experience with sensations of anger, and at least some experience with sensations of relaxation, sensations of self-acceptance may be less common. Fortunately, the definition of self-acceptance is pretty clear—it means loving and accepting ourselves as we are ... *now* ... not as we wish we were. As long as we wish that *anything* were different about us, we are not self-accepting. If we're aspiring to self-acceptance, we can't even get down on ourselves for not being self-accepting—it's a contradiction in terms!

In some ways, the lack of self-acceptance can be considered a subcategory of judging: self-judging. And, ironically, even when we judge ourselves and come out well, we are still judging ourselves, and true self-acceptance implies love and compassion without any judging. This is because self-judging, even when apparently in support of self-esteem, is a fickle friend. Yesterday's success will all too quickly become a standard that we cannot live up to today, thus making us a failure in the eyes of our judging mind!

Of course, lots of people, from politicians to athletes to rock stars, appear to have a great deal of self-esteem—that is, they appear to judge themselves very positively. At least, they try to convince others of just how fine and right they think they are. Sadly but obviously, they must pretend an exaggerated self-love to cover their lack of true self-acceptance. Our goal is to reduce the harsh self-judging that often makes a facade of this type seem crucial to maintaining self-worth. When we really accept ourselves as we are right now, we simply don't need any mask or false front to impress anyone else.

The Experiencing Self-Judging Meditation: Practice

Since thoughts of self-judging and self-acceptance may be less obvious, and thus less easy to recognize, than anger thoughts, we'll start with an experiencing meditation before we do a labeling meditation. And since it may, for many of us, be easier to work towards self-acceptance after beginning to identify and diminish self-judging thoughts, we'll work with self-judging before we tackle self-acceptance.

You can begin to work with these painful self-judging thoughts just as you worked with angry thoughts. Once again, we want to move from saying: "I shouldn't be _____" or "I'm not a very good person" or "Everyone's better at _____ than I am" to: "Ah yes, a self-judging thought is coming into my mind."

First, as you did in the meditation on page 110, bring a self-judging thought into your mind. Without even trying to bring acceptance to the issue represented by the thought (for example, excess fat), simply let the thought become the object of your focused attention. Then alternate a few seconds of focus on the self-judging thought with a few seconds of your favorite mind-clearing meditation. After a few alternations, you'll probably find that the self-judging thought feels less painful, as it just becomes another "thing" to look at in the mind.

A tremendously useful variation of this exercise is one in which you visualize yourself using meditation to soften around the pain of the self-judging thought. Like the sparring drills of the karate student, the more you practice under controlled conditions, the better you'll be able to apply meditative skills to real-life self-judging thoughts.

The Self-Judging Labeling Exercise

As you did in the Particular Thought-Counting Meditation (page 86) and with your angry thoughts, set aside a period of time in which you agree with yourself to label self-judging thoughts whenever they occur throughout the day. Are they frequent? Rare? Try to notice (it might even be useful to write a few notes down) when they tend to occur: At home? At work? When you're busy? Not so busy? Under stress? Relaxing? When you think about other people? Are they associated with any other thoughts or actions? Can you identify any thought chains that lead to thoughts of self-judging?

The Experiencing Self-Judging Meditation: In Real Life

When you're ready, go back to the previous exercise. But instead of just labeling, or thinking about the circumstances under which self-judging thoughts occur, wait until one pops up, then try to make it the focus of your attention for a moment. Is anger part of your self-judging thought? Envy? Fear? Do you experience resistance to the very idea of looking at this type of thought? (Join the party!)

Use the technique of alternating a moment of focusing on the self-judging thought with a moment of your favorite meditation. Continue to look for thought chains or situations that seem to trigger self-judging. Whenever a desire to judge yourself for being self-judging arises, alternate back to the meditation, and it will probably subside. And beware of allowing self-judging thoughts to linger in your mind under the guise of self-improvement. Recognize that the old "But I have to judge myself! How else will I improve?" is just one more way of launching a sneak attack on self-acceptance. Self-acceptance means right now. As you are. It doesn't mean (as I explain on page 110) that you won't work to change or improve conditions internal or external. It does mean that you'll try to do so without negative, self-judging thoughts.

Working with Self-Judging

As with thoughts of anger, becoming aware of the thought chains or circumstances that lead to thoughts of self-judgment will help you to deal with those thoughts. So will developing the ability to soften around both the pain of not being as you wish you were, and the pain of not being self-accepting.

As in all of the softening around pain exercises, this involves relating to the thought in your mind rather than getting caught up in the content of the thought. Which as we know is easy to do. It may help to try to remember that the pain of self-judging (self-hate) is a deeper pain than the pain of the surface condition causing the self-hate (overeating, or sloth, or zits). Using a few moments of Compassion Exercise (page 104) may help to remind you of this. So may a moment of thought on the Master Skill, since the ability to accept yourself no matter what is far more important than the ability to hone your mental or physical or financial facade!

Working with Self-Acceptance

In addition to working with our reaction to thoughts of self-judgment, we also want to encourage thoughts of self-acceptance. As you did with an external circumstance in the exercise on page 112, bring a thought of yourself into your mind, and, just for three minutes, view yourself mentally with no judgment. Every time a self-judging thought slips in ("Just look at those hips!" or "I should have studied more this morning . . . "), soften around it with your favorite meditation. The more you cultivate a sense of self-acceptance under practice conditions, the more you'll be able to apply it during the day. In fact, after you've done this exercise a number of times, you may want to try substituting a moment of self-acceptance meditation when a self-judging thought arises, instead of using your usual favorite breathing exercise.

If it's hard for you to be self-accepting for even three minutes, please work with any of the compassion exercises as often as you can, then return to this one (perhaps right after doing a few minutes of compassion meditation).

Self-Acceptance and the Master Skill

In some ways, maintaining a sense of self-love no matter what happens *is* a form of the Master Skill. Because if you really love and accept yourself, you won't need to impress, intimidate, or attract other people. So chances are that you'll lead a pretty compassionate and aware life, a life fine just as it is.

Fears and Phobias

What Is Fear? What Is a Phobia?

A standard dictionary might tell us that fear is an emotion caused by the expectation of danger, or that phobias are irrational behavior patterns that result from one's reactions to fear. But the truth of the matter is that fears are nothing but thoughts, and phobias nothing but our counterproductive reactions to those thoughts.

Perhaps the most unpleasant thing about the way we react to fear is the manner in which it seems to expand to fill our entire mind and body. Yet, like any other thought, we can make room in our mind for fear, enough room to focus on it as just another object in awareness, just another thought. We can even learn to use fear, when it arises, as a reminder of our need for mindfulness and compassion.

The Fear-Labeling Exercise

Most of us probably don't have much trouble identifying fear thoughts. They're pretty obvious. But we may not always notice the circumstances under which they tend to appear, and we may not be aware of thought chains that lead to fear thoughts. So it's most likely worthwhile to do a fear-labeling exercise a few times, just as you did the anger labeling (page 143) and self-judgment labeling exercises (page 151) in previous sections.

Working with Fears and Phobias

A fairly successful type of psychotherapy for dealing with both fears and phobias is called systematic desensitization. A typical program of systematic desensitization might involve teaching a person who has a terrific fear of spiders, for instance, to do a relaxation technique similar to the one on page 99. After the person has learned the technique, the therapist would then expose the person to a *very mild* form of his or her fear object, perhaps a cuddly toy spider, or a cartoon of a spider, or even a picture of a different bug. As the person began to react fearfully, he or she would be encouraged to use the relaxation technique. After a number of repeated fear/relaxation sessions, the mild form of the fear object would no longer frighten the person. At this point, the therapist would introduce a slightly more threatening version of the fear object (perhaps a photo of a spider) to be used in the next set of fear/relaxation sessions.

Fear/relaxation sessions would then be held with an increasingly threatening series of fear objects, until the subject could successfully practice the relaxation techniques while watching a live spider at close range.

Meditation can be used similarly. In fact, that's very much what you've been doing when you bring an angry thought into your mind, then soften around it with a moment of your favorite meditation. And, of course, the same thing can be done with thoughts of fear. However, with very powerful fears or phobias, creating a graded series of fears to soften around (as the therapist above did for her client) is apt to be less stressful than trying to start right off by softening around the worst possible case of your worst fear.

The Difference Between
Fears and Phobias

The difference between fears and phobias is the same as the difference between thoughts and emotions (page 157). A fear is a thought caused by the expectation of a real or imaginary danger. A phobia is a behavior pattern that we develop when we habitually overreact to a particular fear type of thought. Phobias often take the form of an intense avoidance behavior—a fear of airplane crashes develops into a phobic refusal to fly, or a fear of germs into a phobic avoidance of shaking hands.

Of course, the diagnosis of a phobia, or of phobic behavior, is somewhat open to interpretation. Twenty years ago, anyone who refused to eat commercially grown vegetables because they were reacting to their fear thoughts about pesticide contamination would have been labeled as the victim of a phobia. Today, that same behavior might be considered no more than a sensible health precaution (and the purveyors of high-priced organic produce would surely agree). As the old joke goes, "*I* take realistic precautions, *you* have a phobia."

Fortunately, fears and phobias are both the result of not being able to control reactions to thoughts in the mind, so both can be remedied by meditation. Let's begin by working with fear.

The Experiencing Fear
Meditation: Practice

As you've been doing in the above sections, bring a thought or image into your mind that usually causes you to "become afraid." Don't feel that you need to begin working with your deepest and darkest—feel free to use a minor hobgoblin, at first. If you find yourself getting caught up in the fear (like Groucho Marx getting mad), alternate the observation of the fear with a moment of meditation, and soften around the fear.

Observe the physical sensations that arise. Does your breathing get more shallow? More rapid? Does any part of your body tense up? What else can you notice?

Now see if you can observe any other thoughts, either preceding, following, or occurring at the same time as the fear thought. Even a fragment of a memory, from childhood, or a prior painful experience, would be interesting to notice now.

Do this exercise a few times, then try it with a slightly deeper fear (but not necessarily anything too threatening yet). Don't forget to do some Meditation Visualizations (as on page 96), in which you visualize yourself softening around the fear, and just watching the mind without getting caught up in its movie.

The Experiencing Fear Meditation: In Real Life

Go back to the Fear-Labeling Exercise on page 153, but this time try not simply to notice and label, but to notice and observe an actual, real-life fear as it occurs. Since you are increasingly aware of *when* fear tends to arise for you (due to practice with the labeling exercise), with luck you'll see the fear coming before it hits you full-blown. Once again, try to observe fear without reacting by becoming fearful, just as an anthropologist observes the customs of a strange tribe without getting caught up in them. If you begin to "feel fearful" as you watch your mind, you know what to do: meditate.

Through meditation, I've pretty much overcome the severe case of hypochondria that had plagued me since grammar school. Occasionally a hypochondriacal thought will still arise ("Oh no— that's *gotta* be rabies!"), but I rarely get caught up in it, even when I'm tired and under deadline pressure (which is when such thoughts are, I now know, most likely to appear). I see 'em coming, and they're almost like old friends whom I don't much care for now. It's as though The Beaver sees Eddie Haskell coming down the street thirty years later—he's someone to be greeted with friendly nostalgia, but not to be trusted, and by no means anyone with whom you'd want to get involved. "Ah yes, hypochondria—I remember you! Bye-bye, now!"

The Experiencing Phobias Meditation

I don't recommend trying to *purposely* work with phobias, or very strong fears, until you've had lots of practice with lesser fears. (Of course, if a deeply fearful thought comes into your mind un-bidden, as they usually do, why not try some meditation on it— you can always scream, run, or bite your fingernails later!) But if you feel ready to do so, this exercise or the following one may help you to deal more skillfully with phobic behavior.

At a time when you are already feeling fairly calm, do your favorite meditation for a few minutes. Then, keeping an investigative spirit, bring your phobia into mind (if you have more than one, choose the one that seems least scary to you first). As I've said, a phobia will usually be composed of fear thoughts about some issue, which you react to by strenuously avoiding certain behavior.

For instance, perhaps you suffer from one of the most common phobias—a fear and avoidance of speaking in public. If that's the case, gently visualize yourself avoiding a situation in which you might need to speak in front of a group. Observe the fear thoughts that arise. They might include a fear of not knowing what to say, a fear of stammering, a fear of blushing, a fear of appearing foolish. Can you identify any thoughts of shame around avoiding the situation? Thoughts of relief? Other thoughts? What if the situation were slightly different—if you had to speak for only two or three people, or if you were asked to appear on the evening news? Just observe your visualizations, like an experienced zoologist might examine a series of unknown beasts, with curiosity but little fear. What can you learn from looking at them? If you find yourself reacting to the fear thoughts and feeling anxious, don't struggle with the fear, just return to your favorite meditation for a moment, then end the exercise for now. Return to it whenever you feel ready, in an hour or a day or so, once again attempting to maintain that air of interested but slightly detached curiosity.

Working with a Phobia: Practice

After you've spent some time gently experiencing your phobia, you'll be ready to create a graded series of visualizations to soften around. This series should begin with a visualization that feels only *very slightly* threatening, and end with one that seems very threatening at present. Most people find that a phobia visualization series composed of from six to ten of the graded visualizations works best.

In the example of public speaking, you might begin with a visualized scenario of yourself reading a one-sentence written message to two friends, without making eye contact. If you begin to feel anxious while picturing this in your mind, immediately return to your favorite meditation. If alternating between the visualization and the meditation does not allow you to create a clear visualization without a lot of fear, choose an even less threatening scenario.

Once you can alternate between the visualization and the meditation without much fear, create a slightly more threatening scenario. Just adding eye contact and an extra listener to the first scenario might be enough for now. Continue to alternate between this visualization and meditation until you no longer experience much discomfort.

By the time you've "escalated" through six or eight more scenarios in a similar manner, you might be visualizing yourself delivering a short, memorized, talk to a dozen friends or coworkers.

Working with a Phobia: In Real Life

If the visualization work with your phobia doesn't feel too stressful, you *may* want to experiment with it in a real-life situation. Simply set up a situation (preferably with people who know of your phobia) in which you recreate the first (and least stressful) of your visualized scenarios from the previous exercise. Make sure it's a situation in which you have the power to end the fear-producing scenario abruptly, if necessary, and meditate before, during, and after the experiment.

If you are unable to overcome your habitual avoidance behavior this time, try setting up a less threatening scenario. If you did overcome your avoidance behavior, try doing so a few more times without increasing the intensity of the scenario. If it continues to feel okay, try to recreate the next of your graded visualizations in real life. But remember—be compassionate with yourself—no one ever "machoed" themselves out of a phobia. Go slowly, and do lots of self-acceptance and compassion meditations as you work with your phobia. You're much better off accepting yourself with the phobic behavior, than being phobia-free but self-judging or uncompassionate!

Fear and the Master Skill

When you can look at a fear thought, and keep your heart open with compassion for yourself, for that fearful being, you're practicing the Master Skill. Because it's really not a life free of all fear that you seek—it's a life in which you are able to deal with fear whenever it arises. And the techniques in this section will help you to do so, if you use them.

Loss and Bereavement

What Is Loss?

Singer Grace Slick once advised her listeners never to cry over losing anything that wouldn't cry over losing you. That's probably good advice, but hard to take, since grief is the pain we feel around loss, and there are many different types of loss. Some losses are internal, like the loss of your self-image as a youthful person, or the loss of idealism. Others are external, like the loss of a job, the loss of money, the loss of a relationship. And although we can grieve over any loss, the greatest loss is the loss of a loved one through death.

Yet even the pain of this greatest loss is still due to thoughts in the mind, and, as thoughts, they can be workable. Saying this emphatically does *not* mean that we "shouldn't" grieve, or that we need to control our grief thoughts.

The story is told of the great meditation master, Marpa, whose disciple found him weeping over the death of his son. "But Master," said the disciple, "You always teach us that death is an illusion. Why are you crying?" And Marpa answered, "Yes, death is an illusion. And the death of a loved one is the most powerful and painful illusion of all."

Marpa was honoring his need to grieve, even though as a meditator he was aware of his ability to control his reaction to his thoughts. It's perhaps the greatest challenge that a meditator faces, but we can learn to do both, with clarity and compassion.

On Working with Bereavement

It would be facile (if not condescending) for me to say that it's as easy to deal with thoughts and feelings about the death of a loved one as it is to deal with even such powerful thoughts as anger or fear. In fact, grief thoughts following a death are often so painful and unmanageable that I recommend working instead with thoughts about lesser losses first. However, we usually can't control the degree of loss to which we will be subjected, so after talking about dealing with smaller losses, I will offer two ways in which to work with big losses and bereavement.

The Loss-Labeling Exercise

If you like, feel free to adapt the other particular thought labeling meditations from the above sections for use with thoughts about loss. This may be especially useful if you think you may have feelings of loss that you are not too aware of. But since most thoughts around deep loss or bereavement are all too obvious, you may prefer to use the Experiencing Loss Meditations instead of this one.

The Experiencing Loss Meditation: Practice

As you've done with other types of thoughts, bring a thought of something or someone you've lost into your mind, and explore it. You may want to begin doing this exercise with an object (a favorite toy or article of clothing that's long gone). Then try it with something that you used to believe in, but have lost faith in (Santa Claus? Socialism? Ronald Reagan's "Morning in America"?). If you feel up to it, experience the thought of having lost a pet, or a friend.

Do the different losses feel different? How so? Do you feel sad? Lonely? Afraid? If you find yourself getting caught up in the loss thought (and thus losing the ability to observe the original thought), alternate it with a moment of your favorite meditation, to soften around the thought.

Don't forget to use this set of thoughts as the basis for a Meditation Visualization. Beginning with the smaller losses, picture yourself softening around the pain of the loss. When you can picture softening around the pain of a small loss, go on to the visualization of a more painful loss, and soften around that one. If this exercise seems as though it might be very painful, please read the entire section before trying it, and perhaps do some more compassion work (page 101) first.

The Experiencing Loss Meditation: In Real Life

Since we tend to hold losses in our thoughts for a long time, there is not too much difference between this real-life exercise and the practice one. It's simply a matter of using as your loss thought a more recent loss, or one which is still more strongly in your mind. The more painful the loss, the more meditation you'll probably have to do to soften around it.

Remember that, like Marpa, you are not trying to *avoid* feelings of sadness or loss—these are the most human of thoughts, and must be honored. However, you are trying to remain aware, as often as possible under the difficult circumstances, that they are still just thoughts in the mind, thoughts that you can watch, thoughts that you can work with, using the skills that you've learned from this book.

Try to understand that even when strong feelings arise, they are a result of the thoughts of loss, of sadness, of fear, and of anger, and they can be worked with and softened around, as *all* thoughts can be worked with and softened around.

Of course the thoughts surrounding a great loss can be very hard to soften around—big surprise. Here are two different ways of working with bereavement that I've used, in dealing with my own grief and with my grieving clients. If you are facing the pain of a major loss, please try both, to the extent that you are able.

Compassion and Bereavement

Losing a loved one is the most intense emotional pain that a human being can experience. There's no easy way to work with it. But compassion will help. When your heart has been torn open with grief, only compassion for yourself, and for this human condition in which death is such an unavoidable part, will help you to soften around the thoughts of pain, anger, fear, and resentment.

Do the Compassion Exercise on page 104 if you can. If you can't, try the compassion breathing exercises on pages 101-103, or my One-Breath Compassion Meditation (page 136), and try to breathe some softness into your broken heart. Allow your heart to be torn apart, and just keep breathing, and softening around whatever thoughts come up. Don't try to get rid of the thoughts, but try to create some psychic space around them, by breathing compassion into your heart between thoughts. Literally try to take a mini-meditation break every minute, with every breath.

It's hard to believe when in the midst of bereavement, but true: Compassion will get you through times of loss better than having what you wanted will get you through times of no compassion.

If you must deal with intense grief, I strongly recommend two things: working with a good therapist who has had experience with grief issues, and reading Stephen Levine's *Who Dies* (see bibliography). As Dr. Elisabeth Kubler-Ross says, "Stephen's work is magic."

Bereavement and Mind Watching

While applying as much compassion as possible, some people will also find it helpful to use mind-watching techniques to deal with loss and grief. If you have found mind watching to be a good way of working with other thoughts, please feel free to try it with the thoughts of loss and grief that arise as well.

Try, if possible, to alternate this grief thought watching with your favorite meditation and remember to return to one of the compassion exercises often.

As you watch your thoughts, you will probably notice that what we call grief is not a single feeling or emotion. It is likely to be made up of a variety of elements such as anger (at the departed, for leaving), fear (of what will become of us), guilt, loneliness, numbness, and relief, among others. Perhaps you'll be able, at times, to notice, label, and experience your different thoughts as they float through your mind: a moment of loneliness, a moment of agonizing grief, a moment of fear, a moment of numbness. But even more valuable than labeling will be to meet each thought with as much compassion as you can manage.

The Waves of Grief

Grief is usually not a constant state, but instead often seems to occur in a series of waves of greater or lesser intensity. Like labor, in which the mother-to-be must work terribly hard during each contraction but can relax for a moment in between, we can sometimes ride the waves of our grief. If we can be mindful enough to notice the rising and falling flow of our grief, we can then compassionately allow ourselves, without guilt or recrimination, an occasional moment of relative freedom from pain, or even a moment of numbness. This will often provide a tiny respite from the pain of the grieving process.

Even a small break from the pain may enable us to return to our grief work with a bit more room for compassion, a bit more room for mindfulness. And the more compassionate and mindful we can be, the more we can avail ourselves of these tiny pauses or letups. For me, when I was first grieving the sudden loss of my dear friend, Timmy, the rare sporadic moments in which my pain would subside and I was able not to think of Tim for a few seconds or minutes proved to be the foreshadowing of my eventual healing process. And, with time, healing does occur, as I'll discuss more below.

Stages of Grief

It takes tremendous awareness of what is really happening, on a moment-by-moment or even a second-by-second basis, in order to work at all skillfully with the grieving process. And to do so, it is imperative that we try to avoid any preconceptions of what the grief process is, or "should" be. For this reason, it's crucial to understand what the widely misunderstood "stages of grief" or "stages of dying" really mean.

In the late 1960s, Dr. Kubler-Ross's pioneering work on the stages of dying achieved great popularity. This conceptual outline (composed, in order, of Denial, Anger, Bargaining, Depression, and Acceptance) also began to be applied to the grief process. Many people, unfortunately, did not realize that these stages represent not a rigid timetable, but a framework for exploring the ways that people relate to death. And these ways vary greatly. The intensity and range of emotions experienced in grief are highly individualistic. One person may express their grief with a catharsis of tears, another, with a subdued, silent, ongoing pain. No right, no wrong . . . just individuals grieving in individual ways.

Likewise, applying *any* kind of timetable to the grieving process (you *should* be able to get over the death of a friend in a month, and a parent in three months) is an attempt to rigidify a process that is unique to the individual experiencing it. There is only one valid timetable regarding bereavement, and that's that time does heal grief—eventually.

Time of Healing, Healing of Time

Time does heal. It's true, but terribly hard to remember when grieving. When we are completely engulfed by thoughts of grief, it can be nearly impossible to gain enough mental space to look at the process, and to realize that it has a progression of its own, and will eventually fade and then pass. But perhaps this story will help to illustrate how the knowledge that time heals can be used.

Back when I was working at the Haight Ashbury Free Clinic, a client named Alexander once told me of his unusual method for avoiding LSD freakouts (which he used to experience every time he took the drug). But somehow he came up with the idea of writing a letter to himself before each trip, which read: "Dear Alexander—Everything seems weird because you took acid at __ o'clock. Things will be back to normal by __ o'clock. Signed, Alexander."

This note, which he read to himself whenever he began to feel anxious (and which his friends read to him if he got so twisted that he forgot about it), always helped him to hold out until things got better. Although hard to grasp in the midst of grief, the knowledge and belief that time really does heal, no matter how terrible the pain is right now, can help us to trust the process, to allow the grief to occur and unfold at its own pace, without fear that it will overcome us permanently.

Bereavement and the Meditator's Worldview

Some of the grieving people that I've worked with find reading and thinking about the Meditator's worldview to be helpful. If reading these sections in this book feel right, you may also want to read the Watts or Nisargadatta books listed in the bibliography, in addition to Stephen Levine's work.

Loss, Grief, and the Master Skill

Loss and grief are perhaps the most powerful teachers and hardest taskmasters that we will ever know. They are also two instructors that none of us can avoid. By trying to deal with them in a meditative way, we can learn the hardest lesson: that giving and receiving love is all that really matters in this transient world. When we can begin, however haltingly, to use even loss and grief skillfully and with compassion, we have truly started to master the Master Skill.

Loneliness and Emptiness

What Is Loneliness?

Loneliness has different meanings for different people. For some of us, loneliness means that we miss a particular person, from whom we're separated by time or space. This type of loneliness may be considered a form of grief or loss (depending on whether the separation is temporary or permanent), and is thus covered in the previous section.

For others of us, loneliness means that we don't have enough friends or people with whom we can share our thoughts and feelings. Whether we are surrounded by others or in voluntary or involuntary quarantine, we feel isolated and alone.

The Loneliness-Labeling Exercise

Unless your loneliness is so chronic that it is always in the forefront of your mind, it may be useful to learn when lonely feelings come up for you. So spend a few hours or days labeling loneliness whenever you notice it coming into your mind. Can you connect your lonely thoughts with specific times, places, or events? Hunger or tiredness? Visual signals, like seeing other people enjoying each other? Are there thought chains leading to the lonely thoughts?

The Experiencing Loneliness Meditation: Practice

Bring a thought of loneliness into your mind, and examine it. What is it like to be lonely? Does it bring up other feelings, like sadness, or fear, or memories? Is it connected with a desire thought—someone you would like to be with, someone who you think would relieve your loneliness?

If looking at the lonely thought in your mind becomes painful, spend just a few seconds in meditation before returning to the lonely thought. Then observe it some more. Spend at least some time using a compassion meditation to soften around the pain of being lonely. And being lonely can be really painful—so be a compassionate friend to yourself for a moment.

After you've done the above meditation a few times, do a Meditation Visualization with the lonely thought, picturing yourself using any mind-clearing or compassion meditation to soften around the loneliness.

The Experiencing Loneliness Meditation: In Real Life

When you feel ready, start to apply the above techniques you used in practice, to the lonely feelings that come up in real life. It probably won't be too much harder, since lonely thoughts are lonely thoughts, whether we bring them into our minds on purpose or they come unbidden.

Loneliness and Judgment

For many of us, even though we feel lonely, we may be very picky about whom we would allow to end our isolation. Our aloneness then may be at least partially due to having very stringent expectations about our friends or lovers. If we are only willing to form a relationship with others who would aggrandize us, or inflate our self-image, we may find that even if we succeed in locating such models of perfection, we still feel lonely. In fact, seeking perfection in any relationship (even in our relationship with meditation) is a prescription for repeated disappointment.

Working with Loneliness

Loneliness can be dealt with on two levels. On the interpersonal level, we can decide to be less judgmental about our company, and seek others to whom we can give as well as take. There are volunteer positions available everywhere in the country, in hospitals and nursing homes, animal refuge centers and orphanages.

On the level of thought, we can choose to use compassion to soften around our feelings of loneliness, and the judgmental thoughts that may be preventing us from making contact with others.

Loneliness: The Compassion Button

After you've practiced softening around lonely feelings with compassion, you can create a compassion button for yourself, just as you created a relaxation button. Practice bringing a thought of loneliness into your mind, and immediately following it with a moment of quick compassion meditation. As you become used to pairing loneliness and compassion in your mind, your thoughts of loneliness become "compassion triggers," allowing you to instantly soften around the lonely feelings. Once again: You are not trying to remove the feelings of loneliness—you just want to learn to react to them with compassion rather than pain.

What Is Emptiness?

For me, the empty feeling that often accompanies words like "Is this all there is to life?" is a form of *spiritual* loneliness, a feeling of not being connected to anything larger or more meaningful than myself and my own existence.

For other people that I've worked with, emptiness might refer more to their sense of a lack of inner self, a sense, as Gertrude Stein said of Oakland, California, (my publisher's hometown, no offense), that "There is no there, there."

The Emptiness-Labeling Exercise

As you did with loneliness, explore your feelings of emptiness by labeling them throughout the day. See when, where, and under what conditions they tend to appear. Can you detect any patterns? What feels empty?

The Experiencing Emptiness Meditation: Practice

If you are able to, recreate a thought of emptiness in your mind, and observe it. What does it feel like? Is it connected to any other thoughts, or conditions? Do any thoughts typically follow it?

Practice softening around the pain of the emptiness. You may be able to do this by alternating your focus on the emptiness thought with a moment of meditation. Since, as with the Experiencing Loss Meditation, there is little difference between working with the experience of emptiness in either practice or in real life, I'll offer a few more detailed suggestions on ways to heal a sense of emptiness in the Working with Emptiness sections, below.

The Experiencing Emptiness Meditation: In Real Life

Use your emptiness practice techniques to work with feelings of emptiness that arise in real life. Continue to observe when these feelings show up—they may be telling you something. Soften around them, if possible, with a moment of meditation, and try the following suggestions as well.

Working with Emptiness . . . As Lack of Meaning

Many of us have become so caught up in the whirl of late-twentieth-century life that our lives feel full of busyness (business) but empty of meaning. Whether you spend ten hours a day in a demanding service profession, or sixty hours a week as an upper middle management person for the widget factory, with time for little else, your life may actually *be* pretty low on meaning. If that's the case, what can you do to make it more meaningful?

I'd suggest becoming involved in some type of volunteer work (especially a type that involves service towards people), because widening your focus to include helping people other than yourself is a time-tested way to add meaning to your life. And, naturally, stepping up your involvement with meditation as well surely won't hurt!

. . . As Lack of Spiritual Connectedness

Perhaps you feel that your work, and/or your relationships, are reasonably satisfying, but still have empty feelings. If that's your situation, then you probably need more of a spiritual element in your life (that's why you picked up this book in the first place, right?). So I'd recommend doing lots of Three Minute Meditations, checking out some of the books in the bibliography, and perhaps even investing ten minutes a day doing our *MetaPhysical Fitness* program.

Some people find that spending a few minutes reading or thinking about the meditator's worldview, and the way in which we are all connected, helps. Others find that a combination of working with the "I Am" meditations, beginning on page 119, and the Meditator's worldview (page 26) helps them to feel more integrated into the "big picture," and thus less isolated. Try doing some visualizations in which you picture yourself feeling well-connected after doing the above exercises, as well as doing the exercises themselves.

. . . As Lack of Inner Self

If you sometimes have painful feelings of having nothing inside, no core, the I Am section and exercises following (page 119) may be very helpful. Try to track your sense of "am-ness" from your earliest childhood memories up to the present—it may help you to reconnect with the sense of self that has always, however subtly, been present. Remember to use lots of compassion exercises, if facing your empty feelings directly is painful. And be aware that the more you practice the basic mind-clearing meditations, the easier it will be for you to do the more advanced "I Am" work. Also try visualizing yourself softening around the pain of the emptiness by thinking about the Meditator's worldview and doing the "I Am" Meditation. If the sense of emptiness has been long-lasting or very painful, it may be skillful to work on it with the help of a good therapist, especially one who integrates meditation into his or her practice.

Loneliness, Emptiness, and the Master Skill

Like grief and death, loneliness and emptiness are parts of being human. Thus, we may never be able to eradicate them from our lives. But if we can use them to motivate our search for compassion, connection, and meaningfulness in our lives, we are, as Nisargadatta says, "Building our bridges from the very boulders that seem to block our path." Which is a very nice way of saying that we are practicing . . . the Master Skill.

Control Issues

What is "Control"?

Webster's dictionary defines the word "control" as: "to exercise restraining or directing influence over, to have power over." But alas, like reading about such things as swimming or emotional intelligence, knowing the definition of the word doesn't help us at all in working with this subtle and complex issue.

Some emotions that pose issues for us, like fear, grief, and anger, are easy to identify, though hard to handle. Others, like self-acceptance, emptiness, or issues around control are less obvious, less easy to pinpoint. Yet, as I've said, all emotions have this in common: They result from thoughts. If there are no thoughts, there are no emotions or feelings. If we can notice the thoughts that precede them, we can work more skillfully with these issues or emotions.

Types of Control Issues

There are a multitude of things and circumstances that we may wish "to have power over," as Webster's puts it. Projects, people, the weather, politics, our bodies, and our minds. Some of us feel a need to control the way we appear to others. Others want to control events. Some want to control friends, lovers, and relatives (this one is so popular that the next chapter, "Codependency," will be devoted entirely to it). Yet regardless of the particulars, a sure sign that control is a problem is if you have an exaggerated negative response when things "just aren't going as they *should*."

Certainly most of us love the sensation, as the song says, of "ev'rything going my way." But those of us who have a high control need are likely to experience either anxiety, anger, or depression (or some combination of these) when we find that we cannot be "in control." Noticing unpleasant emotions like these, in conjunction with mental phrases such as "but it" or "they *should* (do X, Y, or Z)" or "everything's going wrong" or "things aren't working out like I wanted," can often help to identify subtle, or not so subtle, control issues. Note the italics on my "shoulds"? This word is often a good hint that control issues are lurking.

Identifying Control-Need Situations

If you feel as though "being in control" may be a problem for you, think about a few specific ways or situations in which you find yourself craving control. At work? At a party? When you have to wait unexpectedly for something? Driving? At a meeting?

If this is hard to do, look at some situations in which, for no obvious reason, you seem to become anxious, antsy, angry, or depressed. Could there possibly be a control issue behind these feelings? Bring one of these situations into your mind, do a mini-meditation to relax, then see if any control feelings or mental phrases like those mentioned above pop up.

The Experiencing Control Needs Meditation: Practice

If you've identified a control-need situation, do your favorite mini-meditation once again, then visualize your chosen situation as clearly as possible. Observe any feelings that arise. Notice any desire to get caught up in the content of the thought, instead of just watching it.

I often use my driving control needs for this exercise. I hate inconsiderate drivers, especially those that travel at extremely low speeds on a two-lane highway without pulling over for me to pass. If I bring an image of this into my mind, I often find myself saying, "But they *should* pull over." In other words, I'm saying to myself that it's not my control problem, it's their bad behavior—because the world (including its drivers) *should* behave in a certain way. Wrong! So I notice that an erroneous-belief thought produces a thought that justifies my control need, then I take a break for my mini-meditation (often a single Compassion Breath), before returning to my thought watching.

Continue to alternate mini-meditation with visualization of your control-need situation. Shift back and forth at least a few times a minute, to make sure that you don't get caught up in the content of the control situation ("But the engineering department *should* get those specs back to me within a day!"). Notice any thoughts, especially belief thoughts about "what *should* be." After a few alternations, you'll likely find it easier to soften and relax around the negative feelings that arise when you are not in control but wish that you were.

Beliefs About Control

For many of us, there is an unspoken belief even more general, and destructive, than any specific belief about the way things *should* be. This is the thought that we *should* be able to control events, people, and our own bodies. When we cannot, negative self-judgment creeps in. So it's also useful to notice judging thoughts during the exercise above. If they do arise, see if you have some unrealistic beliefs about the nature of the world. Because, sadly, the reality of control is that there really isn't any.

If it were easy to manipulate the world with any degree of assurance, quotes like "Man proposes, God disposes" or "The best laid plans of mice and men gang aft agley (trans: go often astray)" would not exist. Think that you *should* be in control? You aren't. You can't be. So the self-acceptance exercises in the chapter of that name may help.

Is "Control" a Dirty Word?

Certainly there are many different types of control, and many different ways of causing ourselves pain around each of them—I know, since I have personal experience with lots of them! But control does not have to be a bad word.

For example, I often use the term "mental self-control," by which I mean the ability to apply various meditation techniques to the mind and its thoughts (like Clearing the Mind, Watching the Mind, Compassion, and so on). I consider this to be a fairly benign use of the word *control*, since I make it very clear (I hope!) that if you're using your lack of meditational perfection to beat yourself up with, you're on the wrong track!

Generally, control becomes a problem when we are no longer simply *trying* to control thoughts, other people, or events. Control issues are only painful when we are either attached to our success in controlling, or (inevitably) hurt by our inability to control, or both. When we get better at recognizing our need to control and identifying control thoughts as they arise, we can be both more compassionate about these needs and more accepting of the generally uncontrollable nature of human existence. Then control becomes more of a skill than a pain-producing issue.

Two General Control Issues

Though an oversimplification, it may not be inaccurate to say that there are two general control issues—no matter how many specific ones may exist. Most of us who have problems with control suffer from both.

The first is the pain that arises from our need to be in control (which, by the very nature of the world, is often impossible). As with all pain, mental and physical, this can be soothed by the application of compassion, and the technique of softening around pain.

The second is the pain that comes from being attached to success in controlling. This can be a subtle pain, since it seems as though it can be avoided simply by learning to be good at controlling. So those of us who are good at controlling may be encouraged to invest even further in our control abilities. But, once again, the nature of the world ensures that this strategy of success through control is a temporary one at best. The following two exercises may help to deal with these two general control issues.

Compassion and the Need to Control

Those of us who have the most need to be in control are often also in the most need of compassion. Control needs, as I'll discuss in the next chapter, often come out of a childhood experience of powerlessness, or worse. So treating yourself, in a compassion exercise, as a child that you love can be a powerful antidote for control needs.

Relax with a mini-meditation, then choose one or more of your most common "control-needing" situations. Visualize it clearly, then do one of the short exercises from the Compassion section whichever is easiest for you. Alternate between the two for a few minutes.

After you've practiced this a few times, try using a Compassion Button (as described on page 169, in the "Loneliness and Emptiness" chapter) with the trigger of a control-need thought. Whenever you notice a control need arising (which will become easier after you've done the first exercise in this chapter), let it be a trigger for a Compassion Button. It's painful to feel powerless. It's painful to need to be in control. These feelings deserve to be treated with compassion, as you yourself do.

If your control needs are so powerful that it's hard to apply compassion to them right now, you may need to first work more with desensitizing yourself around these needs. In the following chapter I'll describe a method (similar to that used in the "Fears and Phobias" chapter) for doing this.

Control Needs and the "Don't Know"

There are times—at work, in relationships, planning vacations—when you will very much want to be in control. Having events work out just as you wish will seem well worth working for, and indeed they may be. But the attachment to control, the need to control, will always produce pain in the end, since eventually every human being loses control, if not now, then in twenty five, fifty, or seventy-five short years.

Balancing the desire for control with the sense of "don't know" can soften your attachment to control. As I said in the "Freedom" section (page 127), we can work energetically towards any end without becoming overly attached to the outcome. So practice the Don't Know Meditation (page 108) whenever you feel a strong need to control a particular situation. If you find yourself saying, "But this really *is* important!" ("and thus it's right for me to be attached to its success"), let that be a signal to remind you of what's *really* important: the Master Skill.

Control and the Master Skill

We can't control our own bodies, let alone other people, or the world. Three bucks' worth of cheap wine in an irresponsible driver, or a particularly persistent bacterium, and all our plans might "gang aft agley." But we can, with diligence and practice, learn to have some degree of "compassionate control" over our thoughts and feelings about control, or anything else. Learning to use meditative techniques to let go of the need to be in control, and of the negative feelings engendered by not being in control, is more important than having "ev'rything going my way." And that, once again, is the Master Skill.

Codependency

What Is Codependency?

The word "codependency" (sometimes written as "co-dependency") has become a label for one of the most common control issues: the need to control the behavior of friends, lovers, or family members.

The term was originally used by the twelve-step group, Alcoholics Anonymous, to refer to a family member of an alcoholic who "helped" or "enabled" the alcoholic to stay alcoholic (by protecting them from the consequences of their drinking—providing money, making excuses, and so on). By the late 1980s, with the publication of Melody Beattie's popular *Codependent No More*, it had come to refer to anyone who, as Beattie puts it, "is obsessed with controlling other people's behavior."

Or as psychologist Anne Wilson Schaef (see bibliography) says: "Co-dependents are supreme controllers." They believe that "they can control other's perceptions (through impression management); control how other people see their families; and control what their children perceive and how they will turn out. . . . All of these attempts to control the uncontrollable lead to tremendous depression, because co-dependents view themselves as failures when they cannot control everything."

Most of us, at least sometimes, wish that we were better at controlling the behavior of others who are important to us. But when this need is extreme, and affects our relationships and our lives, it may have become what I would call a codependence *phobia*.

Though widespread, codependence phobia is very painful and difficult to deal with; working with a trusted and experienced counselor while using this chapter is highly recommended.

Codependent Thoughts and Feelings and the Codependence Phobia

As I've said, a fear is a thought caused by the expectation of a real or imaginary danger. A phobia is a behavior pattern that we develop when we habitually overreact to a particular type of fear thought. Codependence, like everything else, is based on thoughts, and thus can be relieved through meditative techniques. But what are codependent thoughts, and where do they come from?

Many therapists believe that codependence often (but not always) arises during childhood, in a home where alcohol or other chemicals are abused or one in which the needs and feelings of a parent or parents (but often a father) are considered far more important than those of the children. Since the needs and feelings of the children are thus neglected, they are forced to give up their needs and feelings in order to survive and be accepted, and loved.

When children are forced to do this, they often mature with an "emotional vacuum," an emptiness inside. All available energy goes into trying to predict and fulfill the expectations of the needy parent or parents. This often turns into a covert form of manipulation, in which the children attempt to control the parent's behavior in order to gain their acceptance. This is done not by force (since the children are powerless), but by taking responsibility for the parent's needs, feelings, and life in general. Sadly, a child often finds a convenient role model for this type of control strategy in a mother who is in a codependent relationship with the father (more common than the other way around, although that too occurs).

So as with many forms of control, certain underlying beliefs develop. When these children grow up, they often believe that devoting themselves completely to another person, and making that person dependent on them will bring them love or acceptance. These beliefs then give rise to thoughts that will likely involve— you guessed it—controlling another person's behavior by manipulating them through dependency. These thoughts can lead to thought chains, which then produce feelings (such as fear, anxiety, and even depression). The desire to avoid these negative feelings causes codependent behavior. This behavior is apt to affect every aspect of life. It is now a codependence *phobia*.

Believing that you *should* be able to control another's behavior (most often a thankless task) is apt to bring up both anxious and self-judging thoughts and feelings. The emotional vacuum at the center of so many codependent people's hearts may well bring up feelings of emptiness. Angry thoughts are often present, but are disguised, since expressing anger in the original codependent childhood situation was unacceptable, if not dangerous.

Compassionate Control

Like all thoughts and feelings, feelings around codependence are amenable to control by meditative methods. However, since control is so central to the codependent, it's especially important not to allow the mental self-control of meditation to become just another outlet for control needs. Thus the concept of compassionate control is crucial.

When we practice compassionate control, we wish to gain mastery, or control, over some issue, event, thought, or feeling. But we are highly aware of how painful it is to *need* to be in control (regardless of our success at it). This awareness is even more essential in relation to the codependent control need, since that need is so often based on painful childhood experiences. It's also invaluable to remember that adopting the codependent way of life is not a conscious adult choice, but a child's way of surviving a hostile environment. Honor the pain of that child's choice by taking him or her into your heart. If you have not already spent time with the full Compassion Exercise (page 104), please do so now—you will need it, to work skillfully at relinquishing a lifelong habit of codependence.

Compassionate control also requires awareness of the basic uncontrollability of the world, its events, and its inhabitants. So reread, and practice, the Control Needs and the Don't Know Exercise (pages 108 and 179) even before you begin to work on the more specific codependence meditations that follow.

When you become able to acknowledge and treat the pain of needing to be in control, and become aware of and accepting of the world's uncontrollability, you are then free to work and strive with zest towards whatever end seems most important to you.

Identifying Codependent-Need Situations

Begin by identifying control-need situations (if you haven't already done so when you read about this exercise on page 176). Then, narrow down the list by focusing only on those control-need situations that involve people who are important to you. While you may wish that other commuters behaved differently, or feel that you *should* be able to control the nerds in the marketing department, you are probably not in a codependent relationship with them, unless they are very significant to you emotionally.

The Experiencing Codependent Thoughts and Feelings Meditation: Practice

Because feelings of codependence can be so painful, it may be easier to create a graded series of visualizations to soften and relax around (as on page 157 of the Phobia section), rather than attempting to deal with the most compelling or substantive situation first. As described earlier, six to ten steps in a series of visualizations usually work best.

Choose a codependent-need situation that's not too fraught with feeling to start with—perhaps a predicament involving a casual friend with whom you experience control feelings rather than a spouse, parent, or child. In fact, you may prefer to begin this exercise by working with a noncodependent control need (like one involving coworkers, or the excruciatingly slow tellers at the local bank).

As usual, alternate a moment of visualizing the situation as clearly as possible with a moment of mini-meditation. A Compassion Button may be especially useful for these issues. When you can feel a sense of softening around the discomfort of your desire and need to control, you are ready to choose a slightly more painful situation to visualize. Work up in your series until you are able to bring your most painful codependent-need situations into your mind and still keep your heart open for a dose of healing compassion. This may take weeks, months, or years; but your habit of codependence did not come overnight, either. And it's worth the effort of dealing with.

Codependence and Thought Chains

Watching your mind will make it possible to see thought chains that begin with the thoughts or feelings that arise in a codependent control-need situation. While doing the preceding exercise, you may notice other thoughts appearing as soon as you bring the codependent situation visualization into your mind. Anger thoughts, thoughts of self-judgment, and fear thoughts are likely prospects following a codependent visualization.

Just notice these thoughts, and use your thought-labeling skills to name them without getting caught up in the emotions surrounding them. Often, thoughts of loneliness or emptiness may emerge. If they do, review the section by that name, and practice those exercises as well (practice enough three-minute techniques and you won't have *time* to be codependent!).

The Compassionate Codependent Control Button

You may also wish to create a Compassionate Codependent Control Button, or CCCB. By this mouthful I mean a mini-meditation based on the Compassion Button, but includes three extra elements. The first is a sense of compassion for the pain of needing to be in control. The second is a sense of compassion for the pain of not being able to control your loved ones. And the third is a sense of compassion for the pain of that child's choice—the child who was forced to choose long ago a painful way of life that seemed, and was, unavoidable.

When I create a button like this, I try to summarize it in a few words. These might be something like: "Ahhhh—control need.

Ahhhh—can't control. Ahhhh—the child." (The words don't need to make sense to anyone but you, fortunately.) Then I picture those words reverberating in the vast, spacious center of my open heart. With a bit of practice, I can summon this button and its multiple messages quite clearly in a second or two.

Dealing with Codependent Emotions: Real Life

By making a clear and complete list of your codependent-need situations, you can attempt to be especially aware of any codependent or control feelings when in those situations. Then, when a codependent feeling that may arise or a need for control comes up in your mind, you'll be ready to identify it as early as possible, microseconds *before* it can form a thought chain leading to negative emotions. That's the time to push the CCC Button that you've created and practiced using during your visualizations. (This becomes less difficult with practice, like everything else.) And when you do miss the initial codependent thought, and the emotions flood in unexpectedly, look on the bright side: You've probably just discovered a new codependent-need situation to add to your list, so that you can be prepared for it next time!

Codependency and the Master Skill

For many codependent people, the codependent lifestyle has its rewards. Someone always needs you (or many need you, depending on you profession—therapists, nurses, and other helping professionals are often codependent). And it's a habit that has seemed to serve you well, at least to some extent, since childhood. You may never choose to completely free yourself of codependency needs. But that's not really the point, anyway.

The point is that by shining two lights—the awareness of your thoughts, and a sense of compassion for them—onto this ancient habit, you can make an adult, informed choice about how you wish to lead your life. The child that you were was forced into a painful decision. The adult you are today can use meditative techniques to review, and perhaps revise, that choice. And the ability to mindfully recreate your own life—day by day, year by year, and minute by minute—is the Master Skill.

The Rest Is Up to You

Owning this book is a step in the right direction, but *using* it will change your life. *The Three Minute Meditator* has introduced you to techniques that can make meditation an incredibly powerful tool in daily life. Every new moment that arises in your life can now be a point of choice, in which you can *choose* to use these techniques to *investigate* thoughts of fear, anger, or desire instead of just mindlessly *reacting* to them. A moment in which you can choose to live in the now, instead of living in habits of the past or wishes for the future. And most importantly, a new moment in which you can choose to treat yourself and others with compassion rather than judgment.

Of course it's not easy to lead a perfectly meditative lifestyle, in this hectic, busy, world of ours. So we have to be *both* diligent and compassionate with ourselves. A metaphor: Meditators spend a lot of time learning to return to the breath, as soon as we notice that a thought has crept in during our breathing meditations. No blame, or discouragement—we *expect* thoughts to come up, and just quickly and gently return our attention to the breath. Similarly, we have to *expect* ourselves to sometimes act unskillfully, or unmeditatively—without blame, guilt, or self-hatred. Our only job is to try to notice when we have lost the path, and then try to return to it as gently and quickly as we can.

A lifetime of meditation can begin simply by observing this next breath, or thought, and the one after that. Is that a hint? You bet it is—you bet your life!

Bibliography

Beattie, M. 1987. *Codependent No More*. Center City, MN: Harper/Hazelden.

——. 1990. *Beyond Codependency*. Center City, MN: Harper/Hazelden.

Benson, H. 1975. *The Relaxation Response*. New York: Avon

Borysenko, J. 1987. *Minding the Body, Mending the Mind*. Boston: Addison-Wesley.

Cowan, J. 1982. *The Buddhism of the Sun*. United Kingdom: Nichiren Society

Goldstein, J., and Kornfield, J. 1987. *Seeking the Heart of Wisdom*. Boston: Shambhala.

Goleman, D. 1995. *Emotional Intelligence*. New York: Bantam.

Harmon, W. and Rhinegold, H. 1984. *Higher Creativity*. Los Angeles: Tarcher

Kornfield, J. 1985. *A Still Forest Pool*. Wheaton, IL: Quest.

——. 1993. *A Path with Heart*. New York: Bantam.

Kubler-Ross, E. 1969. *On Death and Dying*. New York: MacMillan.

LeShan, L. 1975. *The Medium, the Mystic, and the Physicist*. New York: Ballantine.

Levine, S. 1987. *Healing into Life and Death*. New York: Anchor Books.

———. 1982. *Who Dies*. New York: Anchor Books.

Nisargadatta, M. 1982. *I Am That*. Durham, NC: The Acorn Press.

Rubin, T. I. 1976. *Compassion and Self-Hatred*. New York: Ballantine.

Schaef, A. W. 1986. *Co-Dependence, Misunderstood-Mistreated*. San Francisco: Harper & Row.

Siegal, B. 1986. *Love, Medicine, and Miracles*. New York: Harper and Row.

Watts, A. 1966. *The Book on the Taboo Against Knowing Who You Are*. New York: Collier Books.

White, J. 1980. *A Practical Guide to Death and Dying*. Wheaton, IL: Quest.

Other Resources

How Then Shall We Live is an eight-hour video series featuring Ram Dass, Stephen Levine, and others. It is often shown on PBS, and for information call Original Face Video at (415) 339-3126.

The Inquiring Mind is a quarterly magazine for meditators. It features articles and a calendar of retreats and seminars led by Jack Kornfield, Stephen Levine, Joseph Goldstein, Jamie Baraz and many other fine teachers. Write to: P.O. Box 9999, North Berkeley Station, Berkeley, CA 94709.

The Dharma Seed Tape Library provides tapes of lectures by Jack Kornfield and other spiritual speakers. For a catalog, write to: P.O. Box 66-B, Wendall Depot, MA 01380.

Spirit Rock Meditation Center is home base for Jack Kornfield, and hosts a variety of other spiritual leaders. For info write to: P.O. Box 909, Woodacre, CA 94973

Stephen Levine (with or without his wonderful partner Ondrea) offers workshops on conscious dying around the country. For more information on the workshops that made me a meditator, write to: Levine Workshops, c/o 1615 24th Ave., San Francisco, CA 94122.

Although I've chosen to use the first pronoun "I" throughout most of this book, *The Three Minute Meditator* is actually the result of a collaboration. The contributions of my beloved twin sister, Dr. Nina S. Feldman, were far from limited to the "Why I Don't Meditate Test." Nina was deeply involved in virtu-

ally every aspect of this project, from the organization of the first primitive outline to the editing of the final drafts.

She encouraged me to continue this project during the period when I was simultaneously producing two books, two cassettes, and a full-length video, all focusing on *my* traditional object of

meditation, the harmonica. I would have been quite satisfied to let *The Three Minute Meditator* languish in some backwater file on my Macintosh computer, but Nina was resolute. With her customary charm, she cajoled and prodded me into finishing this book. And the results, quite literally, are in your hands.

So thank you wombmate. . . . Ready to do the next book yet?

Some Other New Harbinger Self-Help Titles

The Headache & Neck Pain Workbook, $14.95
Perimenopause, $13.95
The Self-Forgiveness Handbook, $12.95
A Woman's Guide to Overcoming Sexual Fear and Pain, $14.95
Mind Over Malignancy, $12.95
Treating Panic Disorder and Agoraphobia, $44.95
Scarred Soul, $13.95
The Angry Heart, $13.95
Don't Take It Personally, $12.95
Becoming a Wise Parent For Your Grown Child, $12.95
Clear Your Past, Change Your Future, $12.95
Preparing for Surgery, $17.95
Coming Out Everyday, $13.95
Ten Things Every Parent Needs to Know, $12.95
The Power of Two, $12.95
It's Not OK Anymore, $13.95
The Daily Relaxer, $12.95
The Body Image Workbook, $17.95
Living with ADD, $17.95
Taking the Anxiety Out of Taking Tests, $12.95
The Taking Charge of Menopause Workbook, $17.95
Living with Angina, $12.95
PMS: Women Tell Women How to Control Premenstrual Syndrome, $13.95
Five Weeks to Healing Stress: The Wellness Option, $17.95
Choosing to Live: How to Defeat Suicide Through Cognitive Therapy, $12.95
Why Children Misbehave and What to Do About It, $14.95
Illuminating the Heart, $13.95
When Anger Hurts Your Kids, $12.95
The Addiction Workbook, $17.95
The Mother's Survival Guide to Recovery, $12.95
The Chronic Pain Control Workbook, Second Edition, $17.95
Fibromyalgia & Chronic Myofascial Pain Syndrome, $19.95
Diagnosis and Treatment of Sociopaths, $44.95
Flying Without Fear, $12.95
Kid Cooperation: How to Stop Yelling, Nagging & Pleading and Get Kids to Cooperate, $12.95
The Stop Smoking Workbook: Your Guide to Healthy Quitting, $17.95
Conquering Carpal Tunnel Syndrome and Other Repetitive Strain Injuries, $17.95
The Tao of Conversation, $12.95
Wellness at Work: Building Resilience for Job Stress, $17.95
What Your Doctor Can't Tell You About Cosmetic Surgery, $13.95
An End to Panic: Breakthrough Techniques for Overcoming Panic Disorder, $17.95
Living Without Procrastination: How to Stop Postponing Your Life, $12.95
Goodbye Mother, Hello Woman: Reweaving the Daughter Mother Relationship, $14.95
Letting Go of Anger: The 10 Most Common Anger Styles and What to Do About Them, $12.95
Messages: The Communication Skills Workbook, Second Edition, $13.95
Coping With Chronic Fatigue Syndrome: Nine Things You Can Do, $12.95
The Anxiety & Phobia Workbook, Second Edition, $17.95
Thueson's Guide to Over-the-Counter Drugs, $13.95
Natural Women's Health: A Guide to Healthy Living for Women of Any Age, $13.95
I'd Rather Be Married: Finding Your Future Spouse, $13.95
The Relaxation & Stress Reduction Workbook, Fourth Edition, $17.95
Living Without Depression & Manic Depression: A Workbook for Maintaining Mood Stability, $17.95
Coping With Schizophrenia: A Guide For Families, $13.95
Visualization for Change, Second Edition, $13.95
Postpartum Survival Guide, $13.95
Angry All the Time: An Emergency Guide to Anger Control, $12.95
Couple Skills: Making Your Relationship Work, $13.95
Self-Esteem, Second Edition, $13.95
I Can't Get Over It, A Handbook for Trauma Survivors, Second Edition, $15.95
Dying of Embarrassment: Help for Social Anxiety and Social Phobia, $12.95
The Depression Workbook: Living With Depression and Manic Depression, $17.95
Men & Grief: A Guide for Men Surviving the Death of a Loved One, $13.95
When the Bough Breaks: A Helping Guide for Parents of Sexually Abused Children, $11.95
When Once Is Not Enough: Help for Obsessive Compulsives, $13.95
The Three Minute Meditator, Third Edition, $12.95
Beyond Grief: A Guide for Recovering from the Death of a Loved One, $13.95
The Divorce Book, $13.95
Hypnosis for Change: A Manual of Proven Techniques, Third Edition, $13.95
When Anger Hurts, $13.95

Call **toll free, 1-800-748-6273,** to order. Have your Visa or Mastercard number ready. Or send a check for the titles you want to New Harbinger Publications, Inc., 5674 Shattuck Ave., Oakland, CA 94609. Include $3.80 for the first book and 75¢ for each additional book, to cover shipping and handling. (California residents please include appropriate sales tax.) Allow four to six weeks for delivery.

Prices subject to change without notice.